D0429071

The Power of Experience

The
POWER
of
EXPERIENCE

GREAT WRITERS OVER 50

ON THE QUEST FOR

A LIFETIME OF MEANING

INTRODUCTION BY
Gail Sheehy

EDITED BY
Jeremy Janes

AARP STERLING

AARP Books publishes a wide range of titles on health, personal finance, lifestyle, and other subjects to enrich the lives of older Americans. For more information, please visit www.aarp.org/books.

AARP, established in 1958, is a nonprofit organization with more than 38 million members age 50 or older. The AARP name and logo are registered trademarks of AARP, used under license to Sterling Publishing Co., Inc.

STERLING and the distinctive Sterling logo are registered trademarks of Sterling Publishing Co., Inc.

Library of Congress Cataloging-in-Publication Data Available

*Credits for previously published material appear on pages 229-232.
Best efforts have been made to notify all copyright holders.*

2   4   6   8   10   9   7   5   3

Published by Sterling Publishing Co., Inc.
387 Park Avenue South, New York, NY 10016
© 2007 by AARP
Distributed in Canada by Sterling Publishing
C/o Canadian Manda Group, 165 Dufferin Street,
Toronto, Ontario, Canada M6K 3H6

*Manufactured in the United States of America
All rights reserved*

Sterling ISBN-13: 978-1-4027-4887-5
ISBN-10: 1-4027-4887-6

For information about custom editions, special sales, premium and corporate purchases, please contact Sterling Special Sales Department at 800-805-5489 or specialsales@sterlingpub.com.

To Helena, Ben, and Luke Janes,
and Anna and Siegmund Langegger

Contents

SECTION 3: BY PASSION DRIVEN

SECTION 4: TURNING POINTS

SECTION 5: WISING UP

Jeremy Janes

Preface

It may have looked like I was browsing a Santa Fe bookstore a few winters back, but in fact I was stalking a specific quarry. That particular December happened to be the first of my seventh decade—my 60th birthday had rolled by in late August—and I had embarked upon a seemingly simple quest: Where in the store, I wondered, was the bright and sparkly anthology that celebrated the wisdom and insights accumulated by my graying peers?

The answer was this: It was nowhere. Continuing my search through the spring, I sought out such a collection in independents, in chains, and on the Internet. Ultimately, I concluded, it simply did not exist.

No problem, I thought; I'll compile one myself. And I'll employ my own not-inconsiderable experience to do so. (As Jonathan Swift once wrote, "No wise man ever wished to be younger.")

The filter I applied was brutal, irrevocable, and absolute: Under no circumstances would this collection become *Chicken Soup for the Elderly and Irascible Soul.* So no soup, but much seasoning: I deliberately limited myself to authors who had reached the mid-century mark or more.

What I came up with awaits you in the pages ahead. If you've chalked up any degree of experience yourself, I hope you'll agree that these passages address just how rich, multiform, and (let's face it) useful in a pinch the accumulation of quotidian existence can be. And if you're of a less advanced vintage, I invite you to sample these accounts, real and imagined, of how the gleaming facets—and shattered shards—of a life deeply lived can be layered, over time, to form a prism through which each of us perceives truths that are uniquely our own. That ability to re-examine past moments, and past motivations, through the lens of subsequent events (and the lessons they deliver) is just one of the many powers conferred, I believe, by experience.

May you find your own power, and your own truths, within.

Gail Sheehy

Introduction

The stories in this remarkable treasury will drive you back to your "knowing place," as author Tina McElroy Ansa describes it, "that spot, your gut, your intuitive self." As I read on in Ansa's story, I recalled a conversation I had with my mother on her 75th birthday. It was my 50th year. I guess she decided we were both far enough along in the journey that whatever she admitted I wouldn't hold against her.

"You didn't have a chance," she announced, sitting on the patio of her Florida home.

My mother laughed as she spoke. She was talking about the day of my birth, her first child. She had gone into the hospital on Thanksgiving eve and wolfed down a full turkey dinner, complete with mince pie and an extra ladle of whipped cream. She was ready to do the work of her life, propagating a dream first carried by her own mother across the Atlantic on a runaway voyage from Belfast, Northern Ireland.

"I always thought, well, I'll make it someday, I'll get to be somebody very special," she mused. But both her father and my father had refused to allow her to pursue a career outside the home. The sting was even sharper now, as we both contemplated what might have been. "I really wanted to be a singer," she said quietly. "And I had a beautiful voice. In those days. My mother was the same way—she wanted to be somebody, and she wanted me to be somebody. But I never made it. So I made up my mind that you were going to be the one."

It was an "aha!" moment, both enlightening and humbling. Until then I was under the illusion that I had been the writer and director of my own story. What had emboldened me to pursue the dream of becoming a writer, I thought, was the drive to break free from the constraints that bound my mother, as part of a generation that was kick-starting the women's liberation movement. In my impatience to succeed, I hadn't seen the hidden hands that cupped my destiny: two women, a mother and grandmother, fierce dreamers whose spirit would not be vanquished. How had they managed to remain unseen? I had to shuttle back through years of memories to find the beginning of the story.

AS WE STAND on the mountaintop of midlife and look back at the path we've taken, the stories we tell ourselves change, must change. A narrow field of vision is natural in the growing stages of early adulthood. The story we have been weaving through our younger years, in which the self is hero or victim but in any case center of the world, begins to unravel in the midlife passage. Our self-image becomes shaky. No longer can we hope to be "rescued" by the father or mother. Approaching 50, we become our own fathers and mothers. Only through the development of our psyche in the middle years can we fit our personal narrative into a larger story.

Carl Jung was the first to define this momentous transformation during which we begin to take back the magical powers we projected on our mates and to find evidence of the essential traits of the opposite sex—male competitiveness, female nurturance—within our own natures. Jung warns that we will cling to the false security of the illusions and "truths" that supported our earlier sense of self. "But we cannot live the afternoon of life according to the program of life's morning," he writes, "for what was great in the morning will be little at evening, and what in the morning was true will at evening have become a lie."

Crossing into second adulthood pushes us beyond the preoccupation with self. We are compelled to reexamine the made-to-order persona that gained us points and protection in our earlier, striving years. As we become more certain of the values we stand for—as we hunger to find more significance in the actions we take in the world—we may permit a "little death" of that "false self." If so, we make room for the birth of a new self, one with the "roundedness" of personality that Jung describes as possible only in the afternoon of life.

That is the power of experience.

Our contemporary culture, however, places very little value on reaching this point, our "knowing place." Seldom do we celebrate the richness of experience because that gift is overshadowed by our obsession with the new. The mass psychology that runs through media, entertainment, and our consumer culture drives us to repackage ourselves again and again as new—a thinner, fitter, sexier, cooler, "forever young" version of that self-inflated persona that served us so well when we actually were young. Yet as philosopher James Hillman reminds us in *The Force of Character and the Lasting Life,* "Old is one of the deepest sources of pleasure humans know. Part of the misery of disasters like floods and fires is the irrecoverable loss of the old." Children seem to sense the special power in the knobby hand of a grandparent who points to the sky or the sea and spins a fabulous tale. Many of the stories within this book evoke a beloved elder, now departed, with longing for what Hillman terms their "undemanding compatibility" or with appreciation for a life lesson he or she imparted through the sheer force of character.

What characterizes the stories and poems in this collection, all by writers over 50, is not the omnipotent Me. They are meditations on experiences stored away in the morning of life and dug up years later, the outer shells peeled off, the core seen with the clarity of the afternoon of life. These works differ from the urgent, striving, self-obsessed narratives of younger writers who believe the world should bend to their will. Time is not apparent in youth. The power of experience has not yet taken root.

Memory is a field between dream and experience that we cross again and again. Memories can hold an emotional power over us for years. On later reflection, however, they may lose their power, or shift, as subtly as a shoreline between seasons or as violently as the collision of tectonic plates. The reexamined memory then imparts a new twist to the story. As we take time to recline in our pasts, we may see the significance of people and events in a truer light—even, perhaps, for the first time.

Many of the stories here recall a talismanic memory that has by now become a cherished friend. Or a wake-up call, confronting the writer with what he or she didn't know—or didn't want to know. Truths. As a reader, you may well be inspired to turn over your own fields of memory. If we do the same spadework, we may be able to reframe a crucial recollection and use it as a signpost for the rest of our journey. A reminder of what matters. What endures.

Verlyn Klinkenborg could not understand his father until the younger man acquired a farm of his own, "a few bony acres," which carried him back to a rebellious boyhood in Iowa. There he had grudgingly helped his father do the hard physical chores of farming. "Now, so many years later, I find myself in a new relation to the old story," he writes in *The Rural Life.* "I'm as old as my father was when the shape my young life was taking must have looked most hopeless to him."

As he starts to measure posts and rafters to build a shed, Klinkenborg begins to understand his father in an entirely new way. He comes to realize why building this shed is a way of learning about his father—why propagating what he's learned is a crop that reseeds and extends itself every season.

What does it mean to be a grown-up? Diana Athill tackles that question in her essay from *Yesterday Morning,* evoking the time when, as a 17-year-old British schoolgirl, she broke out of the haze of erotic daydreaming and dared to stand up to the absurd authority of sexual repression. Her moving story reminds us of the intense erotic prelude savored by many girls through their mid- to late teens in the days before peer pressure equated going to bed with being grown up.

In Robert Stone's *Bay of Souls,* a Vietnam veteran wrestles with the faith question upon learning he may lose his young son to exposure from a winter storm. Awaiting the doctor's verdict, incensed by the leaden surrender of his Bible-bearing wife, he confronts the fear that Providence will punish his unbelieving-ness. When his son survives, he is able to accept his own truth—his existential belief in the randomness of life and death. Through the transformative power of this experience, the father feels that he has become, at last, a grownup.

AS FOR ME, it took years to come to terms with my mother's revelation and revise the story in my head.

My grandmother, Nana, was one of six siblings, the rebellious one. She loved to dance and dreamed of becoming a professional dancer, but mostly she wanted to be free to forge her own life. Not for her the forced servitude of most 15-year-old Belfast lasses in her day, dispatched to the linen factory to stand knee-deep in water and soak cloth until some bloke married them so they could spend the rest of their days cooking and cleaning.

When her mother beat her beaux with a stick to drive them from the door, Nana wrote to her Irish cousins in America and told them she was ready to run away. I loved hearing my mother retell Nana's story: the climb out the window in the dark, the blind bike ride down Waterloo Road for miles until she met up with a bus that would take her across the country to a boat that would ferry her across the ocean to be met on some dock in America by a man who had agreed to pay for her passage as his mail-order bride.

"Nothing stopped her," my mother said. "She made of her life what she wanted it to be. Well, almost."

My grandmother did become somebody in her community. She built a summer house for the family to enjoy; she lugged the stones uphill to create a huge terraced garden. And she lived to the exceptional age of 89. But she never achieved her dream of becoming a dancer. The price of her freedom from factory work was a strict husband who forbade her even to think about venturing on stage.

So she invested her dream in my mother.

Imagine the thrill of those two women, conspiring to sneak my 13-year-old mother out of the house to take voice lessons. My mother was gifted with a lovely, lilting voice. Her dream was to be an opera singer, or at least an operetta singer. But her dream, too, exacted a crippling price: When her father found out that Nana was sneaking money to pay for his daughter to study to be a singer, he beat the two women, precipitating a divorce—and a concession that my mother would drop out of high school and keep house for him.

The few voice lessons she took remained indelible. I know, because all through my childhood she sang for me the songs she had learned.

One in particular came to represent for me her special power.

Said the little boy to the little girl,
"Pray, give me just one kiss."
The girl was so surprised,
"You're a stranger, sir," said she.
"I will give you just one kiss
When apples grow on the lilac tree."

The boy felt very sad at heart,
She was the only one;
The girl felt quite remorseful
At the terrible wrong she had done.
The very next morning
he was quite surprised to see
the little girl, standing in the garden,
tying apples on the lilac tree.

That was my mother, always able to make something magical out of the ordinary. Tying apples on the lilac tree.

But when it came to me, look what the poor woman had to work with! A buck-toothed, freckle-faced, flat-chested child who was pronounced, even by my kind-hearted Aunt Minnie, to be "not exactly a looker." Why did my mother bother to give me all those lessons? Sew all those ballet costumes? Listen to me recite the lines for my drama teacher?

Nana, too, got in on the project. She gave me a typewriter when I was seven or eight. Clacking down letters on yellow foolscap and slamming that carriage from left to right to make sentences until I saw the sentences had grown into paragraphs and then into pages, time passing without my even knowing it—yes!—this was my own Atlantic crossing. I could be a woman and not have to bend to men's rules. Writing didn't depend on anyone else. It didn't require one to be pretty.

Unlike many girls who had to live out their mother's vicarious dreams or measure up to inflated expectations, the gardeners of my destiny never let me feel pressured into performing for them. I began to appreciate how my mother and grandmother had simply fertilized the soil by soaking me in culture, literature, and lessons, then letting me choose the path.

I wanted to know more about this alchemy. "When did you begin?" I asked my mother.

"Oh, from the moment you were conceived, I knew you were going to be somebody," my mother insisted. "I had it so fixed in my mind that you couldn't help yourself. I injected it into your DNA, kid!"

My mother's laugh was a cascade of delight. At last, now that her daughter was 50, she was able to claim credit for tying apples on the lilac tree.

I | *Awakening*

"Experience is not what

happens to you; it is what you

do with what happens to you."

— Aldous Huxley

Mary Oliver

The Journey

One day you finally knew
what you had to do, and began,
Though the voices around you
kept shouting
their bad advice—
though the whole house
began to tremble
and you felt the old tug
at your ankles.
"Mend my life!"
each voice cried.
But you didn't stop.
You knew what you had to do,
though the wind pried
with its stiff fingers
at the very foundations,
though their melancholy

was terrible.
It was already late
enough, and a wild night,
and the road full of fallen
branches and stones.
But little by little,
as you left their voices behind,
the stars began to burn
through the sheets of clouds,
and there was a new voice
which you slowly
recognized as your own,
that kept you company
as you strode deeper and deeper
into the world,
determined to do
the only thing you could do—
determined to save
the only life that could save.

Born in Cleveland, Ohio, in 1935, Mary Oliver realized two facts about herself early on that have shaped her life: She found great joy in the natural world, and she wanted to be a writer. At age 15, longing to be a poet but with few female literary role models available to her, Oliver wrote a letter to Norma Millay Ellis, sister of the recently deceased poet Edna St. Vincent Millay, asking if she could visit Millay's estate in upstate New York. Ellis agreed.

Oliver arrived two days after graduating from high school. She became Ellis's secretary, helping to organize Millay's papers. There she also met and fell in love with Molly Malone Cook, who would become Oliver's life partner and literary agent. Together they moved to Provincetown, Massachusetts, in 1964.

Though she attended both Ohio State University and Vassar College, Oliver never received a degree. She left school, in part, because she felt ready to write on her own. Her first collection of poems, No Voyage, and Other Poems *was published in 1963, and she won a Pulitzer Prize for her third book,* American Primitive, *in 1984. In addition to her many books of poetry, Oliver has published prose, including* Rules for the Dance: A Handbook for Writing and Reading Metrical Verse *(1998). She has also taught at several schools, including Bennington College and Case Western Reserve University.*

Shortly after she won the Pulitzer, Oliver described her routine as follows: "I simply do not distinguish between work and play." Private and solitary, she takes long walks daily around her home in Provincetown, jotting down observations about the world she sees. Oliver then crafts these notes into her trademark lyrics of sensitivity and acuity.

"I believe art is utterly important," she once said. "It is one of the things that could save us."

Alice Munro

Hateship, Friendship, Courtship, Loveship, Marriage

In the countryside where I lived as a child, wells would go dry in the summer. This happened once in about every five or six years, when there was not enough rain. These wells were holes dug in the ground. Our well was a deeper hole than most, but we needed a good supply of water for our penned animals—my father raised silver foxes and mink—so one day the well driller arrived with impressive equipment, and the hole was extended down, down, deep into the earth until it found the water in the rock. From that time on we could pump out pure, cold water no matter what the time of year and no matter how dry the weather. That was something to be proud of. There was a tin mug hanging on the pump, and when I drank from it on a burning day, I thought of black rocks where the water ran sparkling like diamonds.

The well driller—he was sometimes called the well digger, as if nobody could be bothered to be precise about what he did and the older description—was a man named Mike McCallum. He lived in the town close by our farm but he did not have a house there. He lived in the Clark Hotel—he had come there in the spring, and he would stay until he finished up whatever work he found to do in this part of the country. Then he would move on.

Mike McCallum was a younger man than my father, but he had a son who was a year and two months older than I was. This boy lived with his father in hotel rooms or boardinghouses, wherever his father was working, and he went to whatever school was at hand. His name was Mike McCallum too.

I know exactly how old he was because that is something children establish immediately, it is one of the essential matters on which they negotiate whether to be friends or not. He was nine and I was eight. His birthday was in April, mine in June. The summer holidays were well under way when he arrived at our house with his father.

His father drove a dark-red truck that was always muddy or dusty. Mike and I climbed into the cab when it rained. I don't remember whether his father went into our kitchen then, for a smoke and a cup of tea, or stood under a tree, or went right on working. Rain washed down the windows of the cab and made a racket like stones on the roof. The smell was of men—their work clothes and tools and tobacco and mucky boots and sour-cheese socks. Also of damp long-haired dog, because we had taken Ranger in with us. I took Ranger for granted, I was used to having him follow me around and sometimes for no good reason I would order him to stay home, go off to the barn, leave me alone. But Mike was fond of him and always addressed him kindly and by name, telling him our plans and waiting for him when he took off on one of his dog-projects, chasing a groundhog or a rabbit. Living as he did with his father, Mike could never have a dog of his own.

One day when Ranger was with us he chased a skunk, and the skunk turned and sprayed him. Mike and I were held to be somewhat to blame. My mother had to stop whatever she was doing and drive into town and get several large tins of tomato juice. Mike persuaded Ranger to get into a tub and we poured the tomato juice over him and brushed it into his hair. It looked as if we were washing him in blood. How many people would it take to supply that much blood? we wondered. How many horses? Elephants?

I had more acquaintance with blood and animal-killing than Mike did. I took him to see the spot in the corner of the pasture near the barnyard gate where my father shot and butchered the horses that were fed to the foxes and mink. The ground was trodden bare and appeared to have a deep blood-stain, an iron-red cast to it. Then I took him to the meat-house in the barnyard where the horse carcasses were hung before being ground up for feed. The meat-house was just a shed with wire walls and the walls were black with flies, drunk on the smell of carrion. We got shingles and smashed them dead.

Our farm was small—nine acres. It was small enough for me to have explored every part of it, and every part had a particular look and character, which I could not have put into words. It is easy to see what would be special about the wire shed with the long, pale horse carcasses hung from brutal hooks, or about the trodden blood-soaked ground where they had changed from live horses into those supplies of meat. But there were other things, such as the stones on either side of the barn gangway, that had just as much to say to me, though nothing memorable had ever occurred there. On one side there was a big smooth whitish stone that bulged out and dominated all the others, and so that side had to me an expansive and public air, and I would always choose to climb that way rather than on the other side, where the stones were darker and clung together in a more mean-spirited way. Each of the trees on the place had likewise an attitude and a presence—the elm looked serene and the oak threatening, the maples friendly and workaday, the hawthorn old and crabby. Even the pits on the river flats—where my father had sold off gravel years ago—had their distinct character, perhaps easiest to spot if you saw them full of water at the receding of the spring floods. There was the one that was small and round and deep and perfect; the one that was spread out like a tail; and the one that was wide and irresolute in shape and always with a chop on it because the water was so shallow.

Mike saw all these things from a different angle. And so did I, now that I was with him. I saw them his way and mine, and my way was by its very nature incommunicable, so that it had to stay secret. His had to do with immediate advantage. The large pale stone in the gangway was for jumping off, taking a short hard run and then launching yourself out into the air, to clear the smaller stones in the slope beneath and land on the packed earth by the stable door. All the trees were for climbing, but particularly the maple next to the house, with the branch that you could crawl out on, so as to drop yourself onto the verandah roof. And the gravel pits were simply for leaping into, with the shouts of animals leaping on their prey, after a furious run through the long grass. If it had been earlier in the year, Mike said, when these held more water, we could have built a raft.

That project was considered, with regard to the river. But the river in August was almost as much a stony road as it was a watercourse, and instead of trying to float down it or swim in it we took off our shoes and waded—jumping from one bare bone-white rock to another and slipping on the scummy rocks below the surface, plowing through mats of flat-leafed water lilies and other water plants whose names I can't recall or never knew (wild parsnip, water hemlock?). These grew so thick they looked as if they must be rooted on islands, on dry land, but they were actually growing out of river muck, and trapped our legs in their snaky roots.

This river was the same one that ran publicly through the town, and walking upstream, we came in sight of the double-span highway bridge. When I was by myself or just with Ranger I had never gone as far as the bridge, because there were usually town people there. They came to fish over the side, and when the water was high enough boys jumped from the railing. They wouldn't be doing that now, but it was more than likely some of them would be splashing around down below—loudmouthed and hostile as town children always were.

Tramps were another possibility. But I said nothing of this to Mike, who went ahead of me as if the bridge was an ordinary destination and there was nothing unpleasant or forbidden about it. Voices reached us, and as I expected they were the voices of boys yelling—you would think the bridge belonged to them. Ranger had followed us this far, unenthusi-astically, but now he veered off towards the bank. He was an old dog by this time, and he had never been indiscriminately fond of children.

There was a man fishing, not off the bridge but from the bank, and he swore at the commotion Ranger made getting out of the water. He asked us whether we couldn't keep our arse of a dog at home. Mike went straight on as if this man had only whistled at us, and then we passed into the shadow of the bridge itself, where I had never been in my life.

The floor of the bridge was our roof, with streaks of sunlight showing between the planks. And now a car passed over, with a sound of thunder and a blotting out of the light. We stood still for this event, looking up. Under-the-bridge was a place on its own, not just a short stretch of the river. When the car had passed and the sun shone through the cracks again, its reflection on the water cast waves of light, queer bubbles of light, high on the cement pilings. Mike yelled to test the echo, and I did the same, but faintly, because the boys on the shore, the strangers, on the other side of the bridge scared me more than tramps would have done.

I went to the country school beyond our farm. Enrollment there had dwindled to the point where I was the only child in my class. But Mike had been going to the town school since spring and these boys were not strangers to him. He would probably have been playing with them, and not with me, if his father had not had the idea of taking him along on his jobs, so that he could—now and then—keep an eye on him.

There must have been some words of greeting passed, between these town boys and Mike.

Hey. What do you think you're doing here?

Nothing. What do you think you're doing?

Nothing. Who's that you got with you?

Nobody. Just her.

Nnya-nnya. Just her.

There was in fact a game going on, which was taking up everybody's attention. And everybody included girls—there were girls farther up on the bank, intent on their own business—though we were all past the age at which groups of boys and girls played together as a customary thing. They might have followed the boys out from town—pretending not to follow—or the boys might have come along after them, intending some harassment, but somehow when they all got together this game had taken shape and had needed everybody in it, so the usual restrictions had broken down. And the more people were in it, the better the game was, so it was easy for Mike to become involved, and bring me in after him.

It was a game of war. The boys had divided themselves into two armies who fought each other from behind barricades roughly made of tree branches, and also from the shelter of the coarse, sharp grass, and of the bulrushes and water weeds that were higher than our heads. The chief weapons were balls of clay, mud balls, about the size of baseballs. There happened to be a special source of clay, a gray pit hollowed out, half hidden by weeds, partway up the bank (discovery of this might have been what suggested the game), and it was there that the girls were working, preparing the ammunition. You squeezed and patted the sticky clay into as hard a ball as you could make—there could be some gravel in it and binding material of grass, leaves, bits of twigs gathered at the spot, but no stones added on purpose—and there had to be a great many of these balls, because they were good for only one throw. There was no possibility of picking up the balls that had missed and packing them together and throwing them over again.

The rules of the game were simple. If you were hit by a ball—the official name for them was cannonballs—in the face, head, or body, you had to fall down dead. If you were hit in the arms or legs you had to fall down, but you were only wounded. Then another thing that girls had to do was crawl out and drag the wounded soldiers back to a trampled place that was the hospital. Leaves were plastered on their wounds and they were supposed to lie still till they counted to one hundred. When they'd done that they could get up and fight again. The dead soldiers were not supposed to get up until the war was over, and the war was not over till everybody on one side was dead.

The girls as well as the boys were divided into two sides, but since there were not nearly as many girls as boys we could not serve as munitions makers and nurses for just one soldier. There were alliances, just the same. Each girl had her own pile of balls and was working for particular soldiers, and when a soldier fell wounded he would call out a girl's name, so that she could drag him away and dress his wounds as soon as possible. I made weapons for Mike and mine was the name Mike called. There was so much noise going on—constant cries of "You're dead," either triumphant or outraged (outraged because of course people who were supposed to be dead were always trying to sneak back into the fighting) and the barking of a dog, not Ranger, who had somehow got mixed up in the battle—so much noise that you had to be always alert for the boy's voice that called your own name. There was a keen alarm when the cry came, a wire zinging through your whole body, a fanatic feeling of devotion. (At least it was so for me who, unlike the other girls, owed my services to only one warrior.)

I don't suppose, either, that I had ever played in a group, like this, before. It was such a joy to be part of a large and desperate enterprise, and to be singled out, within it, to be essentially pledged to the service of a fighter. When Mike was wounded he never opened his eyes, he lay limp and still while I pressed the slimy large leaves to his forehead and throat and—pulling out his shirt—to his pale, tender stomach, with its sweet and vulnerable belly button.

Nobody won. The game disintegrated, after a long while, in arguments and mass resurrections. We tried to get some of the clay off us, on the way home, by lying down flat in the river water. Our shorts and shirts were filthy and dripping.

It was late in the afternoon. Mike's father was getting ready to leave.

"For Christ's sake," he said.

We had a part-time hired man who came to help my father when there was a butchering or some extra job to be done. He had an elderly, boyish look and a wheezing asthmatic way of breathing. He liked to grab me and tickle me until I thought I would suffocate. Nobody interfered with this. My mother didn't like it, but my father told her it was only a joke.

He was there in the yard, helping Mike's father.

"You two been rolling in the mud," he said. "First thing you know you gonna have to get married."

From behind the screen door my mother heard that. (If the men had known she was there, neither one of them would have spoken as he had.) She came out and said something to the hired man, in a low, reproving voice, before she said anything about the way we looked.

I heard part of what she said.

Like brother and sister.

The hired man looked at his boots, grinning helplessly.

She was wrong. The hired man was closer to the truth than she was. We were not like brother and sister, or not like any brother and sister I had ever seen. My one brother was hardly more than a baby, so I had no experience of that on my own. And we were not like the wives and husbands I knew, who were old, for one thing, and who lived in such separate worlds that they seemed barely to recognize one another. We were like sturdy and accustomed sweethearts, whose bond needs not much outward expression. And for me at least that was solemn and thrilling.

I knew that the hired man was talking about sex, though I don't think I knew the word "sex." And I hated him for that even more than I usually hated him. Specifically, he was wrong. We did not go in for any showings and rubbings and guilty intimacies—there was none of that bothered search for hiding places, none of the twiddling pleasure and frustration and immediate, raw shame. Such scenes had taken place for me with a boy cousin and with a couple of slightly older girls, sisters, who went to my school. I disliked these partners before and after the event and would angrily deny, even in my own mind, that any of these things had happened. Such escapades could never have been considered, with anybody for whom I felt any fondness or respect—only with people who disgusted me, as those randy abhorrent itches disgusted me with myself.

In my feelings for Mike the localized demon was transformed into a diffuse excitement and tenderness spread everywhere under the skin, a pleasure of the eyes and ears and a tingling contentment, in the presence of the other person. I woke up every morning hungry for the sight of him, for the sound of the well driller's truck as it came bumping and rattling down the lane. I worshipped, without any show of it, the back of his neck and the shape of his head, the frown of his eyebrows, his long, bare toes and his dirty elbows, his loud and confident voice, his smell. I accepted readily, even devoutly, the roles that did not have to be explained or worked out between us—that I would aid and admire him, he would direct and stand ready to protect me.

In a clear reference to the school of literature that produced Eudora Welty, Carson McCullers, and Flannery O'Connor, Alice Munro claims to belong to the Southern Ontario Gothic school of writing. She grew up on the outskirts of Wingham, Ontario, where her family struggled to make a living from her father's silver fox farm. It has been observed that the setting where she grew up—neither country nor city—has served as the backdrop for many of her stories, and that it is uniquely ambiguous.

Munro has talked about the presence of real settings, objects, and characters in her fiction, citing as an example a reference to a real ceramic elephant sitting on a mantelpiece. "The fictional room, town, world, needs a bit of starter dough from the real world," she said.

Munro won a scholarship to the University of Western Ontario in 1949, when she was 19, and there she began to attract attention for her writing. One fellow undergraduate who took notice was Gerry Fremlin, a "Byronic figure on campus, dark and lean," as Munro's daughter Sheila put it. Fremlin wrote Munro a letter comparing her to Chekhov, but by the time he wrote her, she was engaged to her first husband, James Munro, who "swooped down like an eagle and carried her off," in Fremlin's words. Twenty years later, Fremlin would become Munro's second husband.

Frederick Busch

A Memory of War

so much depends
upon

a red wheel
barrow

glazed with rain
water

beside the white
chickens

Alex had submitted it to the former Miss Casey, their seventh-grade teacher, who made it clear, with a great smile he would now call girlish, that henceforth they were to address her as Mrs. Coyne, for she had married Mr. Stephen Coyne, known as Fighting Stevie Coyne when, in the Golden Gloves Tournament of several years past, he had "eradicated"—Mrs. Coyne's word—Horace (the Cobra) Diaz, the New Mexican entry, in the welterweight competition held in Portland, Maine. "Mr. Coyne is still tough," she told them, "he is a southpaw, difficult to figure out in a short fight, and gifted with a fast jab as well as a left hook to the rib cage that will do you some damage. But he will tell you that I am tougher. I ask him to take the garbage out, the garbage gets taken out. Am I understood?"

She was tall and very slender—skinny, they called her—but with enough of a figure for the boys to study when she wore her pilled, thin, rose- or milk-colored sweaters with a straight skirt. She always wore penny loafers, and they made her look, from the knees down, like a girl. She hadn't that much of a chin, but Alex always found her compelling. And she knew about books. She gave him novels to read—who, among his few friends, read Rafael Sabatini's *Captain Blood* or Burroughs's *Pellucidar: A Sequel to "At the Earth's Core"*?—and she discussed them with him only if he asked her to, and only so long (she seemed to know) as he wanted to talk.

He thought of it, years and years afterward, as a wish to compel her deeper attention, as if shoplifting to satisfy a stymied child's needs, say, because he was angry that she had married; he felt not only jealous of the love she broadcast, but ignorant of the sort of love that made the tall, cool, competent grown-up sisterly teacher—out of reach but, also, somewhat alluringly close to it—belong suddenly, and so exclusively, to the very mysteriously male and very tough and therefore dangerous Fighting Stevie Coyne.

The assignment, at the beginning of their poetry unit, was to write a poem about something that mattered to them. "It has to matter. It can't just be interesting. You have to *care* about it," Mrs. Coyne told them. "And if you don't care much, then I won't care at all."

The poems were due on an autumn Friday. He remembered how, that weekend, he heard the loss, on his tall, golden radio, of the Lions to the Green Bay Packers. He kept trying to figure out why Paul Hornung's last name was pronounced with an *ing*. He was supposed to be a playboy and a gambler, and Alex expended a good deal of imaginative energy on riddling out precisely what a playboy did. He had spent a lot of Thursday afternoon at the public library with a list of names taken from *Windows into Language,* the high, heavy textbook for their experimental advanced English course. He was looking for something special and he thought he had found it—verse he knew to be incomprehensible to anyone in class, and maybe even to Mrs. Coyne. It seemed serious stuff, and that was what he wished to submit. On Monday, after Home Room, and after Introduction to the Romance Languages, a course in French, Spanish, and Italian that began with a long unit on Latin, for sixteen gifted children and Alex, they entered Mrs. Coyne's room in bright October light. Heat rose about the shellacked pine desks and the chalkboard, the wooden floor that was dull from soapy hot water, the back-wall bulletin board with its thicket of clippings about famous authors—Steinbeck and his dog, Hemingway kicking a tin can—and heat beaming from a red-faced Mrs. Coyne.

She would not look at him, though usually she smiled a greeting, and often enough she might ask him about his weekend. She looked happily at Madeleine Cohn, however, and Alex knew she detested her. Maddy had bigger breasts than Mrs. Coyne, and she didn't seem to mind that a number of the boys nearly drooled when they studied how her blouse or sweater clung. Like several of the girls in the seventh grade, Maddy seemed to Alex to be twenty, while the boys, for the most part, himself included, seemed closer to nine or ten.

"I enjoyed reading your poems," Mrs. Coyne told them as she handed them back. His had no grade. Three kids, he knew, had spotted the sentence written in her high, perfect hand, and they stared at him as if he wore several heads in the collar of his shirt. He started to perspire, and he knew it was not because of the glare of the early autumn sun. PLEASE SEE ME, Mrs. Coyne had written at the top of the page.

"One in particular," she said, "seemed to me to be—I suppose you might call it—professional. It's the work of a master, you might say. Alex Lescziak: will you read us your poem, please?"

He had entered a tunnel of short length. He could see light at either end, but there was darkness about his head and face and shoulders. Although the tunnel was small, his voice was magnified within it, and it sounded hollow. He heard himself as if from a great distance. "So much," he read, sounding to himself like a narrative voice on a slowed-down movie when the film slipped from its sprockets, "depends," he read, as if it were part of a telegram written in a single line, and he leaped into "rain/water" and collapsed among "white/chickens" and sat down, his head beating like a heart, pretending to study his creation anew.

"What's the poem about?" Mrs. Coyne asked.

As his vision cleared, he awaited his classmates' insights.

"Alex," she said, "I asked: what is the poem about?"

"Me?" he said.

"Stand, Alex, will you?"

"Yes," he said, standing with his hand on the top of his desk so that he would not fall over. "It's—farming. It's about agriculture. You need to have water to have a good farm, and you need to take care of the farm tools and all, and, you know, you need, you know, chickens and such."

Her mouth moved, and he thought, for a blessed instant, that she would give him a broad smile. She did not. "Chickens and such," she said.

"I was thinking about cows," he told her. "My father used to work on a farm when he lived in Europe, and he told me about cows. Lots of farmers choose to raise cows instead of chickens. But some," he said, swallowing a mouthful of saliva that felt hot and that seemed to sting, "will choose chickens. I'm not sure why, really."

"Interesting," Mrs. Coyne said. "An agricultural poem, then."

He nodded.

"And the lack of capital letters?"

He thought of an FBI story he had read in which the stalwart G-men caught a kidnapper with the help of their laboratory experts: you could trace a typewriter through the way it typed; no two machines were alike, according to the FBI. "The typewriter," he said to Mrs. Coyne. "It's my father's old portable from England, from when they lived in England after Europe, and the thing for capital letters doesn't work."

"The shift," Mrs. Coyne said.

"The shift," he agreed.

"As in 'shifty,' I suppose. And is there anything else we ought to know, Alex?"

He got cocky because untruth might have been working to set him free. "Well," he said, "the word 'glazed' is a pretty unusual word. When

I used it, at first, I thought it meant like glass, you know?" He had, by then, turned to face his classmates, declaiming, moving his hands through the air as if he had something to say and a way he might say it. They looked at him as if he'd been sucking helium from balloons and talking in a Donald Duck voice. "But I figured I didn't mean that at all. What I was *really* getting at was how the water kind of *coats* the, ah"—he consulted the poem on his desk—"the wheel barrow. Yeah." They looked at him with amusement, but also with a kind of horror. He understood, then, that they were watching Mrs. Coyne's face, and it was commenting on his commentary. "I think that's all," he said, without looking at her, as he sat down.

She then asked Madeleine Cohn to read her poem. Even though it was Maddy and her pink oxford shirt, he could not look at her. He remembered her sweet, deep, lisping voice as it chanted something about autumn ending with winter and things getting cold, which is like your grandfather dying. His grandparents had died before he had met them, and he could not imagine winter now. He could not, in fact, imagine surviving the day. So he stared at his poem and its innovative use of "glazed," and then he looked at the ceiling. If one of the huge, milky glass globes that hung from its metal rod connected to the ceiling would only snap, he thought; and if it chanced to be the one that hung above the head of Mrs. Coyne; and if he could leap from the bench of his desk and dash across the room to tackle her, while cushioning her head from contact with the wooden floor; and if the globe shattered harmlessly behind them; and if she looked up into his face and understood that he had saved her—then something like one more day of his life might be attainable.

But the light globes shone, floating above them, and the danger in the room belonged to him alone. Class went on, then class ended, and the next group of students entered. Mrs. Coyne packed her zippered portfolio and motioned Alex to follow her. They went to a room he had only heard about, small and dark, where teachers sat in shabby chairs, like the ones in his living room at home, and smoked cigarettes and read newspapers or, like fat, short, smelly Mr. Delaplane, who also did this everywhere else, stared in front of him like he was watching a terribly sad television show. She led Alex to a little desk with a couple of chairs at it. Nobody sat there, and he figured it was the place you dragged cheats and told them they were getting suspended from the seventh grade.

She sat and sighed, reached for an ashtray, and lit a cigarette. He was thrilled to watch her crimson lips close around the end of her L&M, then slowly release and expel the stream of smoke. He felt as though he watched her getting dressed in the morning.

She said, "That was a brilliant defense in there, Alex." She let a big grin open, and then she shut it down and took another drag. "But you lied. You cheated. I read that poem, you smart little son of a bitch. I used to love that poem. And you spoiled it for me. And let me point out, if I may, that it was *not* because of its high agricultural content that I once liked it. We could have spoken with a great deal of profit about imagery and how you might try *not* saying the obvious in a piece of writing. Or about the importance of seeing the thing itself as a way of doing honor to the world. Because I think of you as having a gift, and I would have enjoyed discussing something that is not predictable doggerel and… Oh, Jesus," she said. "And young. If only you had written it, Alex. Do you know who did?"

"I forget," he said. "Double-u Cee Someone."

"And that's the third of your sins." The hand holding the cigarette, which looked long and glamorous to him, pointed at the fingers of the other hand. "You cheated. You lied to me. You failed to give a real poet, named William Carlos Williams, the credit, much less the praise, he deserves." Alex was thinking of the sleekness of her fingers as they danced to the tune of her condemnation. He did not care about a poet named Carlos Anyone. And he wondered, now, in the parochial-school class-room, if some of the amusement that tugged at her mouth was not pro-voked by her sense that he had possibly been sufficiently enchanted by her—even if he'd underestimated the range of her reading—to risk his academic neck in the theft of a poem that might impress her. All these years later, he was grateful, he thought, for the latent sexuality she'd both felt for and extracted from him.

He remembered startling himself and her by saying, "I hope that you and Mr. Coyne are very happy."

She had somehow understood him. "We are, Alex, thank you. And I would like you to meet him someday. He and you could be friends."

He nodded, having been shown his place. He was grateful, anyway, to survive, as he thought then he might.

"You must write a poem of your own," she said. "Tonight, for tomorrow morning, in my home room, at half past eight. It must be a very good poem. Do you understand what a very good poem has to be?"

"Not about chickens," he said.

She leaned her face in close to his. He smelled the perfume of her breath: the dark secrecy of her mouth, the moisture that made her tongue gleam, and the spiciness of tobacco. "No," she whispered, "not about chicken *shit*. I want the genuine article from you, Alex Lesczaik. No lies. No trying to impress the teacher as if she were Madeleine Cohn with her… endowments. I want you to impress the *Muses*. To say something you couldn't otherwise say."

"Okay," he told her, although he was utterly confused.

"You do that all your life," she said.

"I will," he promised.

"Try, anyway," she said. She stubbed out her cigarette and reached to lightly slap his cheek. "Now: shame on you. Work honestly. And thank you for the compliment."

He said, quite brilliantly, "Huh?" as she led him from the lounge.

So what *then,* in light of his near-death experience in seventh-grade English, led him, later that afternoon, to kick through orange and yellow leaves on their short front walk, and climb the brick steps of their stubby stucco porch, and, entering the silent house, shuffle through the ragged-ended papers stuffed, but not yet fastened, into his three-hole looseleaf notebook, and climb the noisy wooden stairs to find his mother and show her his poem? He must have still thought of it as his. He had attempted with it to woo a teacher he didn't understand he wished to woo. But she had understood that he did. And she had signaled him all of that without saying so, quite. And the secret of poetry, she had told him, was to say something that he could never otherwise say. And there he was, more than thirty years later, trained and habituated to analyze statements unsaid. Toting a guilt that seemed somehow, by then, heroic, he went from one unavailable woman to another, bearing all that he then possessed that might pass for tribute.

His mother wore, he remembered, a very dark, full dress, perhaps

the color of coffee without cream, fastened at the neck and somehow decorative in a way that had to do with pleats and folds. It was
what she wore when his father begged her to accompany him to
something at the university. There was a reception for graduate students, he remembered, and she ought already to have been there,
serving tea from a samovar and smiling, according to her description of her responsibilities at these events. He was pleased to find
her lying on her bed, on the left-hand side of the room, with a pillow over her head. She pulled it aside as he knocked at their bedroom door.

"A headache," she said, smiling a little. "The other pillow, you are
thinking, why? Because it is cool on face, at top of the head."

"Forehead," he said.

"Exactly. Of course. You are well in school?"

"I wrote a poem," he said, standing beside her.

"You are giving it to me?"

"Showing it. If you like."

She sat up, making the furrowed face with which she always demon-
strated her pain, her sacrifice in not submitting entirely to it. "Give,"
she said.

"You didn't go to the tea."

"The pain in the head," she said, slowly shaking her head. "He is
understanding."

"He understands, Ma."

"Of course. Give."

He handed her the poem, and she slowly followed its lines. He
watched her finger trace the extra spaces of the breaks as Williams had
carved them onto the page. And then her face brightened. She lost the
sallow, sad tones he was used to. She smiled with the face of someone
else. That person faded soon, but he had seen her, and he knew that he
had seen something rare and would remember it. *"Barrow,"* she said.
"What is the importance, in a poetry in America?"

"Poem."

"Of course. *'Poemat,'*" she said. *"Gedict."*

"Huh?"

"Old words, foreign. Long time ago, when I was girl, nearly, and you were baby. A person giving me *Gedict*, he called it. We were saying in Polski *Poemat*. We don't talk it no more. Anymore," she corrected herself. "And this?" She pointed to Mrs. Coyne's crimson injunction.

"I stole the poem." He wanted to lay his head on her stomach, on the fancy, scalloped dress she was supposed to be wearing for his father at his school. He wanted to weep. He wanted to shout cruelties about himself, and about her and her blunted, staggering language which never, unlike his father's, had improved. "Somebody else wrote it. I didn't write it."

"Not Barrow?"

"I didn't write *any* of it, Ma! I cheated!"

She sat up higher, then leaned back against the headboard, wincing. "What are you meaning?" she asked.

He heard himself in school as he chattered his clever drivel about agriculture. "Nothing," he lied or confessed. "Nothing."

"Meaning bad? Good? Nice? Not nice? What you are *meaning*. At what? No: who. I am confusing, now."

"I don't know. You should have said confused."

"Of course," she said. The skin around her eyes looked moist now, and her face was softer than usual. "This I am knowing."

"What?"

"From long time ago. You are being good. You are meaning good, baby boy. Come. Come."

She embraced him at the edge of her bed, and he smelled the lushness of the soaps and perfumes and lotions she applied to herself. As his body lay against hers, his feet still on the floor, he thought of Maddy Cohn, and he thought of Mrs. Coyne. He did not think of William Carlos Williams nor, with any understanding, of what, from the submission of the poem to his return from school, he had been meaning to mean.

"I am knowing this," his mother said.

"I *know*, you say it, Ma."

"Of course. Of course. But this: maybe is love in someone, Alex. Stealing poetry, giving to someone—"

"Maybe it's love, you say."

She said, "Of course." She rubbed the same cheek that Mrs. Coyne had pretended to slap. And she smiled. And she looked like the old ladies in half a dozen brown-black photographs his parents had taken with them from Poland and rarely examined. She smiled, and she said, imitating her child's brusque tones, his boy's cracking voice, "Maybe it's love, you say."

In an early incident from A Memory of War, *the 21st novel of Frederick Busch, his protagonist, psychologist Alex Lescziak, recalls a grade-school cheating incident and his teacher's unusual punishment: the challenge to write a real poem. Busch once described to an interviewer a similar real-life incident, in which a fourth-grade teacher praised a poem he had written about a dogwood tree. The realization that he could create something that would "placate and seduce what I can of the world... so that it might smile on me" inspired him to become a writer.*

History—and its repercussions—is a central theme of much of Busch's work, and factors into A Memory of War *through an intricate plot in which Lesciak must confront the appearance of a half-brother who claims to be the result of an affair between Lescziak's Jewish mother and a German SS officer. It is this memory—or the suppression of it—that brings on the headaches his mother suffers.*

Born in Brooklyn in 1941, Busch taught literature and creative writing at Colgate University in upstate New York from 1976 until his retirement in 2003. He died in 2006.

John Edgar Wideman

Hoop Roots

I could take you there… show you the exact place on Finance Street in Homewood, Pittsburgh, Pennsylvania, where fifty years ago playground basketball began for me, and what would you see. Stand with you on the vacant side of Finance where nobody lives and look through a rusty fence that separates the unpaved sidewalk from a steep hillside overgrown with weeds and stubby trees, whose flat crest bedded railroad tracks when I was a kid and trains still run there and a busway too now, ferrying Homewood people back and forth from downtown Pittsburgh, point through the rusty webbing of twisted wire to a level expanse of ground along the foot of the hillside where no trace remains of a building that once occupied the empty space you see there today, the only structure on this side then, no fence, just this big shedlike building on our negro street where white men arrived to work every weekday, cramming their cars and pickups helter-skelter on the hillside, the bottom row's wheels straddling the curb.

Standing here, we are not far from the T-junction terminating

Finance Street at Braddock, an avenue named for a Revolutionary War general, a dead white man as much a stranger to me once upon a time as the white strangers who worked in the factory or warehouse or bottling plant doing whatever they did in the only building on the track side of Finance, a block and a half from Braddock Avenue, three and a half from Homewood, the other avenue bracketing our short street backed flush against a jungly hillside. Finance a street easy to miss if you blinked after the dark, echoing underpasses on Braddock and Homewood below the train tracks, delivering you here to a community most Pittsburgh people thought of as the wrong side of the tracks, this street marking the beginning and end of the neighborhood in which I was raised, where I used to look for trains in the sky, a street dividing so-called black people from so-called white people, where basketball began for me.

My grandmother's house, 7415, and everybody else's on Finance—Smiths, Conleys, Colberts, Berts, Clarks, etc.—faced the tracks. With my chest pressed into the back of the sofa beneath the front room window, just tall enough on my knees to see out, I'd daydream away hours, waiting for the next train's rumble to fill the house, rattle the window glass I liked to frost in winter with my warm breath and draw on, airplanes, horses, moon faces with slits for eyes, crying eyes that shed real tears when I stroked them right, rivers of tears dripping all the way down the pane, ghost eyes and streaks still visible when the women did their spring cleaning and my grandmother hollered, Look at all this mess, boy. Better stop that scribble-scrabbling on my windows.

No matter how far forward you leaned over the sofa's back, you couldn't see the building farther up the block, on the opposite side of Finance, I could lead you to today and show you where it all began, where fifty-some years ago at a hoop nailed to its outside wall I touched a basketball first time and launched my first shot. And because it couldn't be seen from 7415's front window, the wall, the building were out of bounds. In those days with everybody in the house on edge, a little shaky, a little unhappy because my parents had split up for the first time and we'd moved back to Homewood without my father to live in my mother's mother's house, sometimes it seemed the whole world might be coming apart, especially at 2 or 3 A.M., startled awake by a train crashing through the bedroom walls, me lying eyes wide open for hours worrying about how, piece by piece, anybody could ever put things back together again.

I guess it was easy in that crowded house for everybody to get on everybody else's nerves and I heard a lot of G'wan away from here and play, boy. The words sounding like a prison sentence since going out to play meant occupying myself in the fenced-in back yard or on the porch or sidewalk in front of 7415 so if any adult wanted to check on my whereabouts a loud shout would be enough to get my attention. Just to be sure I wasn't into any mischief, the adult in charge could spy through the front room picture window or the little square window at the back of the house above the kitchen sink. Playing outdoors meant staying close enough so no one ever needed to step out of 7415 to keep an eye on you.

On a good day my mom, grandmother, or one of my aunts might take me by the hand across Finance and let me roam the hillside. Don't you dare try and cross the street till I come back for you. And don't you dare march yourself up near those tracks. Whoever escorted me repeated these commandments and a few others, usually ending with the rule, Better stay where I can see you, young man, or I'll snatch your narrow hips home.

I tried never to be busted for breaking rules because getting caught brought more rules, tighter lockdown, but even in a household of loving, attentive women, an only child, particularly a male child, could slip away. In Homewood boys need to think they can get away with things. And sometimes women encourage boys to believe they can. How else keep alive in their male children the cute, mischievous twinkle racial oppression strives to extinguish. To cut slack for their men, the women made allowance for the fact that boys will be boys. Created space, a license for their men to bend rules, a hedge against demeaning rules. The women required this slack as much as the boys if they didn't want to be nailed down too tightly themselves. But the women also had learned from bitter experience that they could be accomplices in crimes against themselves, setting themselves up to be sideswiped or demolished by the first and last rule: you can't trust people, especially men and boys wounded by rules, to respect rules.

As a kid I thought women made up the rules and I resented them for it. I also couldn't help noticing that women were more restricted by rules than men. The rule for instance that kept women home all day and night with us kids. Females (though I'd never have thought of calling them *females* or *women* then), my grandmother, aunts, and mother, seemed embodiments of rules and I began to treat them as I treated rules—obstacles to be circumvented, deceived, ignored when I could. If I got caught straying too far out of line, my mother would threaten, Wait till your father gets home. And if and when he did arrive home that day, he might punish me with his hard hand for breaking rules I knew he didn't follow. It seemed to me my father came and went as he pleased. Said whatever to whomever. Closed himself off in the bedroom and nobody better disturb him. Clearly, if I ever grew big enough, strong enough, no one could punish me. I'd be a man, on top like my father, privileged to make my own rules, to slam people for busting rules I wasn't obliged to honor. Men could, perhaps should, I believed, go about their business as if women's rules didn't exist.

I learned I could slip outside the frame of 7415's front window, just so I didn't stay away too long, just so I wasn't invisible when somebody in a bad mood or a big hurry came looking for me. On a tight leash, yes, but it stretched far enough so I could pretend no leash tethered me to the center of the space whose edges I roamed. Part of me, even then, understood that pain-in-the-butt restrictions were linked to being loved and indulged in my grandmother's house and that I couldn't have one without the other. The dread of losing 7415's special sense of well-being, even for a short cloudburst of frowns or fussing or tighter rules, of losing the kisses, smiles, and mostly sweet, untroubled rhythm of my days, usually was enough to persuade me to police myself.

Abiding by the women's rules paid off, but some days, boy, you know what I mean, slipping away exerted an irresistible pull. Whatever sensible purposes the rules served—my safety, the convenience and peace of mind of the adults—they were also a challenge, a dare. They existed to be broken. The afternoon I fired my first shot at a hoop, I was testing as I did daily in a hundred secret games how much I could get away with. In this instance, how long could I remain out of sight of 7415's front window. Visible within the frame a minute, then gone for two, visible again, then absent five minutes, sneaking farther up Finance with each foray and on each trip away longer. I knew whoever was in charge of me would get busy with one thing or another inside the house. Plus, I figured out three facts I could count on. First, I wouldn't be allowed to play on the hillside unless they trusted me. Second, the more I appeared to cooperate, the more trust and less surveillance there would be. Third, the eyes constantly on duty at the window scanning the hillside existed only in my mind. Except for unusual circumstances—my mom maybe, on one of those days when her eyes were red and puffy, her nose sniffling, a glazed-look day when she might sit at the front window or kitchen table and stare for hours at nothing, silent, a force field of hurt so palpable around her you bumped into the sting of its barbed wire if you stepped too close—no adult would plant herself on the couch under the window with nothing better to do than maintain unbroken vigilance on the empty hillside where I was playing.

Once I understood that my imagination endowed the eyes with more power than they deserved, I was ready to begin imagining their absence, begin preparing myself for the great escape, the moment when I could convince myself that I had nothing to fear from the patrolling eyes. Minute by minute, day by day, I stretched my leash a little farther. Coached myself to stay away a little longer. No one's watching all the time. Even if Aunt Sis or Aunt Geral or Grandma Freed peeks out and doesn't see you she'll figure you'll be right back in a second, you're a good boy, they trust you and boys will be boys, so she'll go on about her business and when she checks again, sure enough, there you'll be, or at worst, if she's having a worrywart day, she'll stand at the window a minute or two till you reappear, back safe inside the arc where you're supposed to be. No problem. If she grumbles or cuts her eye at you later—Better stay where I can see you, mister. Don't be getting too big for your britches— a bit of a smile probably in her sideways glance. Boys will be boys.

No problem as long as the scenarios I constructed inside my boy's pea-brained skull more or less matched what actually transpired inside the house. Of course once I ventured out of sight of 7415, anybody behind the glass was as invisible to me as I was to them. I remember thinking yes, it's a window and through it you're able to watch rain and snow, trains shake-rattle-and-rolling past up on the hilltop, see Freed's roses blooming pink and bloody purple on bushes the neighbors begged her for cuttings from each spring, check out odd-looking grownups walking to and from stores on Homewood Avenue, but seeing through a window is also being blind as far as it doesn't allow you to look at what it hides beyond the view it commands. I wouldn't have thought the word *commands* then, probably wouldn't have formulated my idea in words at all, but I know I intuited something very precise about how brick walls and windows could function in the same fashion when it comes to keeping you unaware.

I wanted to explore what might be happening farther up Finance Street so I wished away the watching eyes. Pretended I controlled the appearance and disappearance of adult faces in the rectangle of glass, just as I once believed the moon followed me when I ran up and down the street, believed the moon vacated the sky when I paid it no mind, believed, in the darkness of the Bellmawr show, I could entice June Allyson's blue, blue eyes to glance down from the screen and smile at the brown boy curled in his seat, shyly in love with her.

After my Aunt Geral had deposited me on the hillside I'd stare at her back as she recrossed Finance to my grandmother's house, to see whether or not she looked in both directions for oncoming traffic before she stepped into the street. *Stop, look, and listen,* the rule she recited to me each time she took my hand and crossed me to play on the hillside. I was always a little worried and maybe slightly disappointed when she didn't get hit by a car those times she didn't bother to stop, look, and listen. Once she'd made it safely to the paved side of Finance, I'd turn away, hang around at the foot of the hillside as if I needed time to get my bearings. I might even shuffle a couple fake steps away from the direction I intended to scoot in as fast as I could the instant I decided she'd had time to reenter the house, take a peek at me through the window. I knew better than to turn around like a dumbbell and stare at 7415. Why in the world would I need to know what was happening behind my back. Weren't the dirt, weeds, stones, trees, bushes, and insects of the hillside more than enough to keep my hands busy, my mind occupied.

I pretended, then came to believe, that I didn't need to turn around to see what transpired in the window behind me. I depended on a picture in my mind, my ability to sense the weight of eyes on my shoulders. I drew a square in the empty air in front of me, and it mirrored what hovered behind my back. I could see Aunt Geral's face, see her eyes, unaware that I watched them, gazing at me, then at the scruffy, overgrown hillside, at parcels of cloud in the sky, the emptiness of gleaming rails waiting for a train. My aunt gazing till what's in front of her mingles with what's not there and she stares through it all, past it to the story of whatever she's deciding to do next. I could feel myself becoming transparent, disappearing as her mind fixed on something besides the nephew playing on the hill. As I think back, I can't help comparing my fake view of her in a made-up mirror in the air to her fading view of me, to this view of a fifty-year-old moment flickering on and off in my head while I attempt to represent it for you—*mirror, mirror, on the wall*—I'm imagining reading these words. The you I promised to take by the hand to where it all started, the place basketball began for me.

If I'd sprinted full speed from the spot on Finance opposite my grandmother's house, I bet I could have reached the building where white men were shooting baskets before my Aunt Geraldine could clomp through the house to a sinkful of dishes in the kitchen. Clomp, clomp, clomp, in her mashed-back houseshoes, glancing at the silent phone, running her finger along the grooved edge of the china cabinet with the cut-glass bowl on top. Sometimes she'd sigh, Wish you were a nice sugar-and-spice girl instead of all snips and snails and puppy tails, you nasty rascal, you. Old enough to stick your arms down in these soapsuds and help your auntie with this mess if you were a sweet little girl child.

From my perspective, an eight- or nine-year-old black boy on stolen time who seldom had much to do with white people, the men up the street in a pool of sunshine in front of the only building on the track side of Finance, launching shots at a hangdog, netless hoop, seemed huge and old, but it's likely they were in their twenties and thirties, some probably teenagers. A few had stripped off their shirts. I remember pale flesh, hairy chests and armpits, bony rib cages and shoulders, long, lanky arms. They blend into the faces and bodies of guys I played with on mostly white teams in high school and college. For some reason one wears in my memory a full beard like the fair-haired Jesus on a calendar, his blue eyes following you around the Sunday school room of Homewood AME Zion Church.

The men didn't talk much as they took turns shooting, rebounding. Some lounged in the shade smoking, ignoring the ball and basket. Seven or eight guys total, I think, probably on lunch break. Somebody had nailed a rusty hoop to a board above truck-size double doors adjacent to the building's entrance. A bright summer day but the interior beyond the partly open double doors in deep shadow. Boxes stacked inside. Machinery too. What little I could see, unfamiliar. Nothing I recognized then nor learned later gave me a clue what work the white men who showed up each weekday performed when they weren't outside shooting baskets.

Once or twice as I watched from the curb the basketball bounced toward me and I retrieved it, rolled it back. Can't tell you whether it was a good, tight, regulation-size ball or some scuffed, lopsided, balloony thing they might kick around or clobber with a bat when they didn't feel like shooting. I don't remember anyone speaking to me. And that was fine because it saved me having to answer. I definitely didn't want to say *yessir* or *nosir* to men without shirts throwing a ball at a basket. I'd been taught at home to be polite to all grownups, especially polite, and as close to silent as I could manage without being impolite, if the grownups happened to be white male strangers. Whether these men shooting hoops spoke or not, I knew I'd better be ready with an appropriate form of address, so I was searching my mind for one. Wonder now if one existed. Or was the point to keep boys like me guessing.

Being unnoticed or ignored allowed me to continue observing them from my spot at the edge of Finance where there could have been a sidewalk if anybody had bothered to pave the no-houses side of the street. Since my presence seemed not to matter, I felt comfortably invisible, a ghost who glided into view once or twice, only intruding enough to keep the ball out of the street, guide it back into the circle.

I must have been watching longer than I realized or maybe till that moment I really had been invisible shuttling back and forth from the safety zone opposite 7415's front window because one of them said, Kid's not going to leave till he gets a shot. Here, kid. C'mon. Try one. I wish I could describe the man who called me over because remembering him might demonstrate how conscious we made ourselves of white people as individuals, aware of their particular features, character, the threat or advantage a specific person posed. In a way, the last great campaign for civil rights, commencing in the southern states in the early fifties, during the same period this scene on Finance Street occurs, was a demand, a concerted political movement to secure, among other things, the same attentive, circumspect recognition of us as individuals that I was compelled, at my peril, to afford to this white guy who handed or passed me a ball.

I could say the ball felt enormous in my hands, because it probably did. I could say I was suddenly shy, timid, and they had to coax me from the margin where I'd been silently watching. Say once I stepped onto the smooth driveway in front of the hoop with the ball in my hands and the basket a mile high poking out from a board fastened on a brick wall, I could tell you how great it felt then to pat the ball for the first time, feel it rise off the asphalt back to my hand, the thrill of lifting the ball with both hands, sighting over it at the hoop, trying to get all my small weight under it and do what I'd watched the bigger, stronger, pale bodies do. No doubt all the above is true. I could also say the men laughed at the air ball I bricked up or encouraged me and gave me more shots or I heaved the ball high and straight and true that first time so it banked off the board through the rim, *Two,* and everybody whooped and hollered. Could say any damned thing because I don't recall what happened, only that it happened, my first shot in that exact place under the circumstances I'm relating, me AWOL from 7415's front window, suddenly scared I'd lost track of time, shooting and hauling ass back down the track side of Finance because I'd probably been out of sight way too long. The story enlarging, fact, fiction, and something in between, till I become who I am today, the story growing truer and less true as I make it up and it makes me up, but one thing's sure, the spot's still there on Finance and I've never forgotten my first shot.

The oldest of five children, John Edgar Wideman was born in Washington, D.C. in 1941 but grew up in Homewood, a black working-class community in Pittsburgh that had been founded by his great-grandmother, a runaway slave. The Homewood he evokes in Hoop Roots *was a tight-knit community, but one that he felt compelled to leave behind. "My exile, my flight from home began with good grades, with good English," he wrote in his 1984 memoir,* Brothers and Keepers, *"with setting myself apart long before I'd earned a scholarship and a train ticket over the mountain to Philadelphia."*

At the University of Pennsylvania, Wideman excelled as both an athlete and a scholar. In 1963, the year he graduated, LOOK *magazine called him "The Astonishing John Wideman." He had won All-Ivy League status in basketball and membership in Phi Beta Kappa, and was only the second black American to be named a Rhodes Scholar. After three years at Oxford, Wideman launched his career as a writer, educator, and social activist. He has twice received the PEN/Faulkner Award, and in 1993 he was awarded a MacArthur Foundation "genius" grant.*

The psychic cost of his youthful achievements was something Wideman could acknowledge only much later. "The price I paid for those successes was self-induced schizophrenia, of being severed from my own history," he revealed in 1989. "Teachers, coaches, nearly everyone in the white university environment, urged me to bury my past."

Buried it would not stay. When his younger brother, Robby, was sentenced to life in prison in 1976 for being an accessory to murder, Wideman wrote Brothers and Keepers *to come to terms with his own history. Two years after the book's publication, his 16-year-old middle child, Jacob, received the same sentence for the stabbing death of his roommate on a camping trip.*

The family has pulled together to keep the two inmates part of the family. "If something terrible happens," Wideman has said, "your choice is either to be crushed by it or to carry on. That's a choice all the time. At this point today, and in my work so far, I have tried to suggest that it is worth carrying on."

Gary Soto

The Effects of Knut Hamsun on a Fresno Boy

My writing life began with poetry in 1973, when I was twenty-one and pinching nickels and dimes from an ashtray in the bedroom for my daily bread. But after reading Knut Hamsun's *Hunger*, I saw myself as a prose writer, one of those patient beings who fits sentences together and moves characters across a page. One summer, I started a short story titled "Ronnie and Joey," a tale of two short friends involved in breaking and entering, a common pastime in Fresno. I was twenty-four, thin as a broom, and with a broom-like head of shaggy black hair. I was newly married. My wife and I were living on Divisadero Street at Van Ness Avenue, and she was the one with a job—with the food stamps gone, our money depleted, our equally poor friends tiptoeing and clawing at their own empty cupboards, we had to do something. With my wife off at work, I opted to write a story. While I didn't see *The New Yorker* as its final resting place, I pictured a journal that might pay. I sat at my desk, which faced a small yard, and putting pen to lined paper, I wrote, "Ronnie and Joey were two piss ants living on the edge of poverty in a town where the worse you cried the more people laughed." I studied the beginning, the pen like a lollipop in my mouth. I decided to add more sadness and gave both characters teeth tight as piano keys. I looked out our bedroom window. A bird flew off a clothesline and, seconds later, another took his place, the line still vibrating from the first bird's departure. Surely this was a fit subject for a poem, but I was now into prose, a turncoat in search of a lucrative career.

I got up and went into the kitchen for a glass of water and leaned against the kitchen sink. I narrowed my gaze on a spider and then the spider's web hooked onto a stubby valve on the water heater. When I bent down for a closer look I saw that it was a black widow, the red on its belly like a fleck of paint. I nearly jumped when the spider sucked in its legs and then spat them out and got away before I could whack it with a newspaper. I felt a tingle after that brief encounter. Since I was inside the apartment and the shadows were still cool, I went outside in the hope of raising a sheen of sweat on my brow, a sweat that would oil my skin and relieve me of the tingle called fear. I admonished myself for being affected so by a spider, though I saw a poem there, too—something about death lurking near the pipes of the afterlife. No, it couldn't be just a plain old water heater but something symbolic and heralding danger.

The neighbors in the apartment complex—seven cottages owned by Mr. Ed Belinsky, an insurance salesman who was wealthy but often bedded in one of the small cottages. Our elderly neighbors, all inside, were either sick in bed or sitting in front of their televisions. Ziggy, a Confederate son and, from all appearances, the offspring of Old Man Time himself, was staring at his rose bush, scrawny as a rooster and just as mean with spur-like thorns. It was too early for him to totter on his gimpy legs toward the local bar called The Space, so he let his attention rest on his plants. I would have said, "Good morning," but it would have taken a long time for him to turn and bring up a smile to his blotched face and even longer for him to raise a hand in salute. Instead, I walked to the front of the apartment complex and assessed the cars as they waited at the red light. At the corner, they were wrapped in their own deadly exhaust—or so my vision had it. I made a mental note of this observation and then nearly jumped when I saw a guy I knew from school. He, a *vato loco* and glue sniffer, was crossing the street pushing a baby stroller. I remembered him from Washington Junior High because he had taunted me for carrying my books, he said, like a girl: the books were propped up in my arms, instead of swinging at my side. "You sissy," he sniped, then spit the shells of sunflower seeds at me. Since he was mean as a rodent, I had to look straight ahead and continue down the hallway, books still propped up to my chest but slowly sliding to my side as I moved out of his view. That was in 1967, the year of peace and hippy love, and now, ten years later, he was pushing a stroller, a motherly act, with the fumes of baby crap blowing into his face. I thought of calling him a sissy, he with a stroller and a diaper bag swinging from the handle, but his knuckles were like skulls showing through his skin. As far as I knew, he was still a mean rodent, teeth slightly bucked and hair slicked back and, yes, a tattoo of a spider pulsating on his throat. Our eyes locked. He knew me from somewhere. He knew it could only be from junior high because he never saw the inside of a high school. He didn't say hello or flick up his head, as if to indicate, *"Que pasa, ese!"* He passed, and I got to watch him push the stroller to the end of the block, wait for the light to turn green and— slyly—glance back. He knew me, but from where?

"See you later, mamacita," I said under my breath, but in my heart I thanked him because I knew he was a poem some time in the future.

I turned on my heels and considered Ziggy, who was still staring at the rose bush. I had a feeling that during my time away—eight minutes, ten at the most—he may have smacked his lips, a high energy activity, and pinched his crotch, "lips" and "crotch" being primary concerns for a drunkard. At three in the afternoon he would employ both these parts of his body after making his way to a barstool at The Space, where he would lift a beer to his face repeatedly until his bladder was full. Then, he would head to the men's room, where the stench could bring tears to the eyes of the heavyweight champion of the world. Ziggy was old and feeble-minded. He might have gone into the john and asked himself, "What am I doing here?" then pee his pants and respond, looking down, "Oh, yeah, that's right." Such was the fate of men who ruined their brains with cold grog on warm afternoons.

I returned to my writing desk and reread the start of my short story about Ronnie and Joey, pals because they were short and the world tall as Zulu spears. I had them sketch their plans for stealing from a rich person's house. I had the owner of the house dead from cutting his lawn: no, not the strenuous nature of the work itself, but from the owner's stingy resolve to save a few bucks. I had the owner swirling a gas can. With a shaky hand, he poured the gas into the tank of a lawn mower, which was overheated and viciously hot. The gas spilled on the manifold of the two-stroke engine and flames leaped up and lit the old man's shirt on fire. I wrote, "A carnation of fire grew into a bushel of devilish sparks," and pushed away from the desk to study the image. It was marvelous, I concluded, and then proceeded to drown the old man—on fire, he jumped into the kidney-shaped pool that was as blue as a toilet wash. The old man flailed in the deep end, stirring up waves no moon could tug from the sea. Desperate, he spat out false teeth, which chattered as they descended to the bottom of the pool. He paddled to the edge of the pool, but his once-loyal Airedale nipped at his fingers and all was lost for the man who made his fortune selling gaudy furniture to poor Mexicans. He sank to the bottom of the pool, a snail-shaped hearing aid popping out of his left ear when his head struck the bottom. Shortly after, Ronnie and Joey slithered through an open window, unaware of the death and mayhem outside in the yard.

I laughed as I typed my handwritten scribble, the keys of my ancient typewriter nearly perforating the typing paper with their sledgehammer-like action. I got up and drank water and studied the space where the black widow once lingered, living on dust and the shell of human flesh, some of which was my wife's and mine and some belonging to the previous occupants, all of them dead now and grinning in their snug coffins. Again the poetry would not stop. I drank my water and after such hard work writing prose, I went outside to once again eye the cars, heat shimmering off the hoods. The fierce sun was lowering the citizens of Fresno into one ass-kicking headlock, squeezing out our bodily fluids. I made a mental note about this poetic truth: we were poor souls caught in a headlock of life by a bully who had the lordly high ground. I returned to my cottage and fixed myself a sandwich, which I ate on the couch, my fingers pinching, crab-like, for flakes of potato chips. I drank water, filling up like a camel, and left the house to walk down to the downtown library.

I passed The Space and then another bar called Mi Chante, both of them nearly empty, though flies hypnotically stirred the air. I came upon a dog with his tongue out. Of course, the poetry took over. I had him walking on his claws, afraid to let the pads of his paws hit the black fry pan of asphalt. The dog, lost perhaps, was wearing a handkerchief around his neck, but I told myself, "No, he's wearing an ascot." I told myself that he was from a good home and was making his way back to his master, but not before a jaunt through inner-city Fresno. What stories the dog would be able to tell his offspring, who, in time, would sport ascots and drink from clean bowls, not the runoff of sprinklers flowing in the gutter.

The library was air-conditioned and the place was packed with people sucking up the cool air for free. Most were children, or people like me, the jobless who would ghost through the shelves and then finally sit down with a previously rifled magazine. I fluttered the front of my shirt. Sweat washed over my chest and its three hairs. My friend Michael Sierra, a poet, worked there, driving the book mobile that stopped at playgrounds and projects. When I asked for Michael at the front desk, the clerk said that he was out making his rounds. So I sat at a table with a globe that was large as a beach ball. I spun the globe and located California. I noticed that its surface was greasy and scratched, every child having tapped a dirty finger on Fresno, their hometown. I got up and drank cold water from the refrigerated water fountain and scanned the poetry section. They were all there, the famous and nearly famous—Robert Bly, James Wright, Adrienne Rich, Diane Wakowski, William Stafford, Theodore Roethke, etc. W. S. Merwin's *The Lice,* then my favorite poetry collection, was there. I picked it up and read a poem called "April," thin compared to other poems but worth studying because I could now argue against its meaning: if you lose nothing, then you learn nothing. I could argue that if a person keeps what is precious, then he or she could wake daily to its shadowy existence and learn something of its nature. Because I was a young man, the poem sounded wise. I closed the book of poems and set it back on the shelf, respectfully, because Merwin was Merwin and wasn't he so deep in poetic meaning that he had to be right?

I left the library and spied Michael parking the bookmobile, the air conditioning on top of the roof humming away as it cooled the shelves of books. I waited for him to park the vehicle, a muscular task of twisting the steering wheel back and forth because he wasn't given much space to nudge that whale into its berth. Finally, he cut the engine and he got out. I asked him, "Let me see the inside?" He let me take a peek into its dark cabin of books, the air still cool, and I was certain that this was the same bookmobile that used to swing around to Romain Playground, circa 1964. That summer I checked out armfuls of books and read them with my face full of apricots snagged from the alley. I told Michael that he had a good job and he sighed and didn't argue but told me he was in a hurry to get out of the sun. I asked him, "Have you read *Hunger?*" and he laughed and remarked, "Nah, I've just lived it."

We both had to laugh. I left Michael in the shade and started toward the downtown mall, skipping over a road embedded with bottle caps and glass, the archeology of poor people. Not far below the road's surface lay teeth and chicken bones—teeth of derelicts and chicken bones from people who ate on the run.

I encountered another dog, this lowly fellow not sporting a red handkerchief around his neck. But like the previous dog, this one was walking on his claws, fearful of the hot asphalt. His nose was black as tar and his throat surely teeming with fleas and ticks. I considered the dog and how God placed him in front of me. I looked at him and he at me, and through our chance meeting understood how each lived off the other's hope. I hoped that in time he would find a place to rest his weary bones before he died. And he had hope in me. I could see that he expected me to bend down and bring my cupped hands to his fuzzy face, bearing water or a half-eaten sandwich. He wanted evidence of human kindness. But what did I have but the salt of writing about Ronnie and Joey, still stick figures on three poorly typed pages. I didn't have much to offer, nothing but a sorrowful glance, and I admonished myself for not being prepared. I hurried away and entered the mall from Tulare Street, which was once a happening place but now full of boarded-up stores. And the few stores still open were poorly stocked and housed mannequins half-dressed, the clothes sold right off their plastic bodies. Music was piped in from speakers hanging at tree-level, but who was there to hear its violins? The birds, I was sure, had by now grown deaf from listening to the canned music.

The fountains were also making their own kind of music, spitting up spines of water, and a few shoppers were swinging their purchases in large bags. A breeze blew between the tall buildings, and the honking of cars echoed off the edifices. I whacked off a few more minutes of life by lowering my hand into the fountain. I wiggled my fingers and then worked them as if I were typing. I want to write a story, I told myself, but I'm thinking like a poet. I couldn't help myself. I imagined that my hand was paddling me into a better life, one with air conditioning and books so refrigerated that when you picked them up, they sent a herd of goose bumps up your arm to your shoulder. Then the hand was a fish, then a tamale dropped by a child into the fountain. I then remembered Knut Hamsun and how he had sat on a bench, touching the brass buttons of his shirt. Hungry, he intended to pawn them, but he was too noble to confront the broker, who would admonish him for being a fool. Instead, he drank water, the universal breakfast for the destitute, and staggered through the cobbled streets of Norway. His mind was dulled by hunger. It was dulled by the undeniable evidence that he was getting nowhere, and, in fact, was slowly disappearing as the pads of flesh melted off his hips. What was I but an offspring of Mr. Hamsun? I was another writer, a poet of many occupations, stirring the water for something good to happen. But since I was wearing a T-shirt, I had no buttons to pawn. If I fingered the inside of my pockets I would have pulled up lint or, perhaps, the teeth of a broken comb.

I yanked my hand out, feeling like a caught fish when I saw the rodent from Washington Junior High. He was pushing his *mocoso* baby in the stroller. I watched him pass under the awning of Lerner's Dress Shop. I began to think like this: truth comes and goes, sort of circulates like those flies at The Space, and eventually lands on what we think is good. Then, when the hand of God waves, we start to circulate again for fear of being struck down by the Almighty. I was doing the same, just moving about, just trying to find the comfort of shade where I could play out that dream of becoming a writer. But then the sun with all its sharp knives appeared and forced me to move.

I left the mall but not before swinging into Longs Drug Store where Hilda, also a junior high classmate, worked the cash register. Penniless, I entered its air-conditioned environs and spied her—she was just lovely, no, better than lovely, a woman with a job. I considered greeting her, but she had customers with red shopping baskets. What would I say? And would she remember me? Me, the boy sitting in front of her in seventh-grade English and telling her that I bought my Levi's, by then faded at the thighs, for $5.45 and what did she think of that? I felt full of pride that day, but crippled many years later as I recalled my attempt at romance. I wish I could have erased that day. "Hilda," I said under my breath, and walked the aisle with shelves of plastic shoes and rubber thongs, Fresno

Birkenstocks, as a friend called them. I held up a pair of rubber thongs and placed them back on the shelf. What was I doing with my free time?

I started my return to the apartment by walking up Van Ness, past a huge, grassy vacant lot, which, twenty years later, I would purchase for Arte Américas, a Mexican art center. If a stranger had stopped me and said, "Boy, you're going to buy that piece of land and make us all proud," I would have thought that this prophet of the implausible future had fallen, hit his head on the sidewalk, and lay there until the sun boiled the noodles in his brains into soft pasta. But I walked past that vacant lot, well, not exactly a vacant lot then but holding out with a single business, a hairdresser. I stopped in front of its steamed window and looked in at two women with huge chrome dryers on their heads. I couldn't help the poetry; in my mind, the women were scorching *their* brains so they could forget their bad marriages and the jugheads they were forced to bed with. The women were lonely and whimpered privately in their cars or behind trees. Although they were heavy with belts of flesh around the middle, they were starved for love. I pressed my face to the window, then turned away when the hairdresser caught me ogling her customers.

The Space was now raucous with workers throwing back their first mugs of beer. Ziggy was seated at the bar, a draft beer set in front of him, and a pretzel around his thumb. It was a little after four. These men would all be dead in ten years, some sooner, and this bar would be gone as well, crumbled by a bulldozer operated by a man who drank there. Another truth: one destroys the place one loves.

I returned to my own place, now lit with the afternoon sun and so blinding that you couldn't look at it without scalding your eyes. I opened the door and a fly rushed to get out; the heat was overwhelming. I flicked on the cooler in the window, which threw out a breeze hot as jet exhaust. I drank water in the kitchen and then, on the second glass, fixed myself a cocktail of ice and tea with two scoops of sugar. I went into the bedroom, where I sat at my desk and drank my iced tea. I wished a pretzel could hang from my thumb. I wished for my own beer, even a flat one dead of bubbles. The breeze from the cooler stirred the few roughly typed pages of my story of Ronnie and Joey. They're coming alive, I thought. I'm making literature! I reached over and picked up Hamsun's *Hunger* and read the back: born in 1859 in Norway, he won the Nobel Prize for literature in 1920. The man was lucky: he got to live in a cold place and win a prize.

In a half-hour, after the cooler pads were moist and refreshing the air, our cottage would be tolerable. Until then, I decided to sit on the front porch and wait for my wife. I had news for her. I was going to tell her that I was through with poetry and that I was going to write a short story about small people whose desire was no more than a good meal and friendship, though first they had to rob a dead rich man's house. I was going to tell her that she was Ronnie and I was Joey, and both of us were going to walk arm-in-arm all our lives.

Award-winning poet Gary Soto was born to a working-class Mexican-American family in Fresno, California, in 1952. When he was five, his father, who packed boxes at the Sunmaid Raisin Company, died in a factory accident, leaving Gary's mother with three children. Gary, the middle child and second son, took any job he could get to help out, from collecting aluminum cans to hoeing cotton and picking grapes and oranges in the San Joaquin Valley—a heritage that has profoundly influenced his writing. In The Effects of Knut Hamsun on a Fresno Boy, *the title essay of his 2000 collection of essays and memoir, Soto likens his lean early days as a writer to the experience of the Nobel Prize-winning Norwegian author Hamsun, who grappled with poverty and near-madness in his 1890 semi-autobiographical novel* Hunger.

The family had no books, and Soto was a D student in high school. "In my youth I had no ambition," he says. "I imagined that I would find a job as a gardener or, worse, as a farm worker with the dullest hoe in the San Joaquin Valley." In 1970, to avoid the Vietnam War draft, he enrolled at Fresno City College. Miraculously (in Soto's own eyes), he didn't flunk out. In his sophomore year he came across an anthology of lively, irreverent poems—by the likes of Allen Ginsberg, Edward Field, and Lawrence Ferlinghetti—that changed his life. "I thought, Wow, wow, wow. I wanted to do this thing," he told an interviewer. He transferred to California State University at Fresno, graduating magna cum laude *with a degree in English in 1974. As early as 1975 his work earned him an Academy of American Poets Prize, and his first book of poetry,* The Elements of San Joachin, *was published in 1977.*

In 1975 Soto married Fresno native Carolyn Oda, the daughter of Japanese-American farmers who had been held in internment camps during World War II. In 1980, their daughter, Mariko, was born. Soto taught literature and creative writing at the University of California, Berkeley from 1984 to 1994. He now teaches writing at the University of California, Riverside.

Rita Dove

Maple Valley Branch Library, 1967

Maple Valley Branch Library, 1967
For a fifteen-year-old there was plenty
to do: Browse the magazines,
slip into the Adult Section to see
what vast tristesse was born of rush-hour traffic,
décolletés, and the plague of too much money.
There was so much to discover—how to
lay out a road, the language of flowers,
and the place of women in the tribe of Moost.
There were equations elegant as a French twist,
fractal geometry's unwinding maple leaf;

I could follow, step-by-step, the slow disclosure
of a pineapple Jell-O mold—or take
the path of Harold's purple crayon through
the bedroom window and onto a lavender
spill of stars. Oh, I could walk any aisle

and smell wisdom, put a hand out to touch
the rough curve of bound leather,
the harsh parchment of dreams.

As for the improbable librarian
with her salt and paprika upsweep,
her British accent and sweater clip
(mom of a kid I knew from school)—
I'd go up to her desk and ask for help
on bareback rodeo or binary codes,
phonics, Gestalt theory,
lead poisoning in the Late Roman Empire,
the play of light in Dutch Renaissance painting;
I would claim to be researching
pre-Columbian pottery or Chinese foot-binding,
but all I wanted to know was:
Tell me what you've read that keeps
that half smile afloat
above the collar of your impeccable blouse.

So I read *Gone with the Wind* because
it was big, and haiku because they were small.
I studied history for its rhapsody of dates,
lingered over Cubist art for the way
it showed all sides of a guitar at once.
All the time in the world was there, and sometimes
all the world on a single page.
As much as I could hold
on my plastic card's imprint I took,

greedily: six books, six volumes of bliss,
the stuff we humans are made of:
words and sighs and silence,
ink and whips, Brahms and cosine,
corsets and poetry and blood sugar levels—
I carried it home, past five blocks of aluminum siding

and the old garage where, on its boarded-up doors,
someone had scrawled:

I CAN EAT AN ELEPHANT
IF I TAKE SMALL BITES.

Yes, I said to no one in particular: That's
what I'm gonna do!

Born in Akron, Ohio, in 1952, the second of four children of Ray and Elvira Dove, poet Rita Dove grew up solidly middle class. Her father, one of 10 children and the first in his family to attend college, earned a master's degree in chemistry. He was the first African American to work as a research scientist for Goodyear Tire and Rubber Company. Both her parents encouraged their daughter's wide reading and dedicated study. In second grade, Dove wrote a novel called Chaos *by taking her list of spelling words and writing chapter by chapter according to the list. She was fascinated to see how the words themselves "would build the reality."*

An achiever on many fronts, Dove played cello in her high-school orchestra and led the school's majorette squad. She was also a 1970 Presidential Scholar and graduated summa cum laude *from Miami University of Ohio in 1973. Fluent in German, she attended the University of Tübingen on a Fulbright Scholarship from 1974 to 1975. In 1977 Dove earned her M.F.A. from the University of Iowa Writer's Workshop, where she met Fred Viebahn. They married in 1979, and their daughter, Aviva Dove-Viebahn, was born in 1983. Since 1989 she has taught at the University of Virginia in Charlottesville, where she holds the position of Commonwealth Professor of English.*

In 1987, Dove received the Pulitzer Prize for Poetry for Thomas and Beulah, *a collection based on the lives of her maternal grandparents. In 1993 she was named Poet Laureate of the United States, the youngest person and only African American to be named to that post. "I think one reason I became primarily a poet rather than a fiction writer," she has said, "is that though I am interested in stories, I am profoundly fascinated by the ways in which language can change your perceptions."*

2 | *Flesh & Blood*

"The dark, uneasy world of family life—where the greatest can fail and the humblest succeed."

—Randall Jarrell

Sharon Olds

7 a.m.

Between the open bathroom door
and the frame, in that tall thin slot of air,
early in the morning I saw my mother's
winter nightie ripple like a witch's.
For a long time she was hidden behind
the wide door, then she glided out,
hunched, miniature, eighty-nine pounds, in
creamy bluish flannel, on her fingers
the sapphires she forgot to take off for bed.
She came over to me and puckered up her mouth
to be kissed good morning. This is the woman who
hit me—she was always a great kisser,
swoonlike and intense. She sits in the chair
beside me, swings her dainty legs,
gazes at me with tender hunger.
I give her a field guide to Western birds,
and she screams, she cannot believe she's receiving

all these species, and in color! She says
she's beginning to understand: there's the moon
and poetry; and now there are birds
and poetry—there's the moon, and birds,
and poetry, and Share. She says,
again, how she did not know it was me
she carried, how could she? How could she know
how proud she would be? Not *proud,* as if it had
anything to do with *her...*
This is the one who took me shopping
for clothes in vertical stripes, for the—uh,
size problem; we'd come back with a nice jail
shirt for me, and some ruffled outfits like a
baby layette for her. She swings her
feet and gazes at me. You have the most
beautiful mouth, she says, it is so
womanly and kind. And the most magnificent
chin, so strong, and yet soft. And then
she shows me what it was like to hit
that High C, effortlessly, in
1934, flinging up
her arms in a victory sign. Her pupilless
medicated eyes are milky blue
as a seer's. I watch her intently: my mother
is a seer. I am a seer's daughter—there is
music, and the moon, and birds, and poetry, and my mother.

"Love is almost the hardest thing to write about," says poet Sharon Olds. *"Not a general state of being in love, but a particular love for a particular person. Just one's taste for that one."* Widely acknowledged as among the most original voices in American poetry, Olds is often described as a "confessional" poet, baring every painful corner of her soul. She will neither confirm nor deny whether her richly detailed descriptions of eroticism, motherhood, and broken relationships are drawn from her own experience, but she has revised some of her poems to remove the names of acquaintances and her own children. *"It's important to me to be able to say that the poems are 'apparently personal,'"* she says, *"so that I can be able to be more free than I can be, to try to be more truthful."*

Personal details are therefore in scant supply. Born in 1942 in San Francisco, Olds will say only that she was raised *"a hellfire Calvinist."* She moved east after graduating from Stanford, got her Ph.D. in 1972, and published her first book of poetry, Satan Says, in 1980. She has won numerous literary awards, including the National Book Circle Critics Award for 1984's The Dead and the Living. She was New York State's poet laureate from 1998 to 2000, heads the creative writing program at New York University, and helped found a poetry workshop for the severely disabled at New York's Goldwater Hospital.

"It just seems to me if writers can assemble, in language, something that bears any relation to experience—especially important experience, experience we care about, moving and powerful experience—then it is worth trying," Olds says. *"The opportunities for offense and failure are always aplenty. They lie all around us."*

Amy Tan

Pretty Beyond Belief

I once asked my mother whether I was beautiful by Chinese standards. I must have been twelve at the time, and I believed that I was not attractive according to an American aesthetic based on Marilyn Monroe as the ultimate sex goddess.

I remember that my mother carefully appraised my face before concluding, "To Chinese person, you not beautiful. You plain."

I was unable to hide my hurt and disappointment.

"Why you want be beautiful?" my mother chided. "Pretty can be bad luck, not just good." She should know, she said. She had been born a natural beauty. When she was four, people told her they had never seen a girl so lovely. "Everyone spoil me, the servants, my grandmother, my aunts, because I was pretty beyond belief."

By the time she was a teenager, she had the looks of a movie starlet: a peach-shaped face, a nose that was rounded but not overly broad, tilted large eyes with double lids, a smile of small and perfect teeth. Her skin bore "no spots or dots," and she would often say to me, even into her seventies and eighties, "Feel. Still smooth and soft."

When she was nineteen, she married. She was innocent, she said, and her husband was a bad man. The day before their wedding, he was with another woman. Later he openly brought his girlfriends home to humiliate her, to prove that her beauty and her pride were worth nothing. When she ran away with the man who would become my father, her husband had her jailed. The Shanghai tabloids covered her trial for months, and all the city girls admired her front-page photos. "They cried for me," she avowed.

"They don't know me, but they thought I too pretty to have such bad life."

Beauty ruined her own mother as well. A rich man spotted my grandmother when she was newly widowed, strolling by a lakeside. "She was exquisite, like a fairy," my mother reported. The man forced the widow to become his concubine, thus consigning her to a life of disgrace. After she gave birth to his baby son, my grandmother killed herself by swallowing raw opium.

Although my mother chastised my adolescent beauty, she sometimes lamented my lack of it. "Too bad you got your father's feet," she would say. She wondered why I had not inherited any of the good features of her face, and pointed out that my nostrils and lips were too coarse, my skin too dark. When I was nineteen, after a car accident left my nose and mouth askew, she told me she was sorry that she could not afford the plastic surgery to fix this, as well as my misshapen left ear. By then I didn't care that I would never meet my mother's standards of beauty. I had a boyfriend who loved me.

In the last years of my mother's life, when she had developed Alzheimer's disease, she never forgot that she was a beauty. I could always make her giggle by telling her how pretty she was, how I wished I had been born with her good looks. She whispered back that some of the other women in the assisted-living residence were jealous of her for the same reason. But as she lost her ability to reason and remember, she also came to believe that my face had changed.

"You look like me," she said. I was moved to tears to hear her say this. Time and age had allowed us to come closer. Now we had the same lines formed by cautious half-smiles. We had the same loss of fat above the innocent eye, the same crimped chin holding back what we really felt. My psyche had molded itself into my mother's face.

Since my mother died, I find myself looking in the mirror more often than I did when I was twelve. How else is my face changing? If beauty is bad luck, why do I still want it? Why do I wish for reasons to be vain? Why do I long to look like my mother?

Amy Tan's turbulent relationship with her mother, Daisy, infuses her fiction, starting with her bestselling debut novel, The Joy Luck Club (1989). Daisy had journeyed to America from Shanghai in 1949 to escape the Communist takeover. In California she married John Tan, an engineer and Baptist minister who had arrived in   1947.

The couple had three children. Amy, the middle child and only daughter, was born in Oakland in 1952. As is often true of second-generation Americans, Tan chafed against her parents' traditional expectations. Especially vexatious to the teenaged Amy were Daisy's rambling and "irrelevant" tales of life in China, her superstitions, her broken English.

When Tan was 14, her older brother and her father died of brain tumors within six months of each other. Daisy fled with her remaining children to Switzerland, where Amy graduated from high school in 1969—and where, grieving and angry, she went wild in rebellion. Daisy soon moved the family back to the United States.

Defying her mother's wishes at every turn, Tan bounced from college to college. The two rarely spoke—except to argue. During one fight, Daisy stung her daughter by revealing a long-held secret: Back in China, Daisy had divorced an abusive husband and lost custody of three daughters when she escaped from Shanghai. Those girls were obedient, Daisy said; they were good daughters.

In 1987 Tan and her mother traveled to China, where Amy met her half-sisters for the first time. Watching Daisy interact with them gave Amy a new perspective. "She was the same with them," Tan said afterward, "both motherly and oppressive and loving and irritating."

The trip transformed her relationship with Daisy. "I saw that my mother was a fascinating person formed by history in a particular time and place," Tan said. "I wanted to know her history." They still fought, but no longer did Tan have to win every battle. "Really, what my mother wants," she said, "is for me to think that what she has to say is valuable. That's all."

Daisy Tan, who suffered from Alzheimer's, died in November 1999 at 83. Hours before her mother's death, Tan learned another secret: Her older half-sisters told her the true names of both her mother and her grandmother. "My mother's many names were vestiges of her many selves," wrote Tan, "lives I have been excavating most of my adult life. What I know about myself is related to what I know about her, her secrets... and with each discovery I had to reconfigure the growing whole."

Sherwin B. Nuland

Lost in America

My father had arrived alone from Bessarabia in 1907, during his late teen years, but youth did not stand in the way of his heroically managing to resist any degree of assimilation. His immunity to the surrounding culture and his avoidance of available aids such as the ubiquitous immigrant night schools of the time has been a never-ending source of bafflement to me, and I sometimes used to wonder whether such an extraordinary feat required a conscious act of will.

I wondered about something else, too, and I will probably always wonder about it. Daddy never spoke of the family he left behind in the Bessarabian town of Novoselitz, nor would he tell us why he did not write to them or they to him. Over the years, I was able to patch together only small bits and pieces of their family history.

The family name means "needle man" (the Yiddish word is pronounced *nuddleman),* or tailor, and like many other European Jewish surnames, it derived from the occupation of a forebear. Meyer's grandfather came from a family of five sons, all but one of whom abandoned their original name of Weinberg. My Weinberg great-grandfather had chosen to rename himself Nuddleman as part of a strategy aimed at avoiding conscription into the Russian army, where Jews faced a mandatory thirty-year period of service without promotion. An exception was made if a family had only one son, who would be permitted to stay at home to help with whatever small enterprise they were engaged in. Nuddleman was the name my father brought with him to the immigration station at Castle Garden when he arrived there alone and virtually penniless. The spelling I inherited was probably the product of an official's attempt to put English letters to Meyer's pronunciation, or it may have made its appearance with the arrival of the two uncles who had preceded him.

What the Weinberg boys did in order to escape the hardship of enforced military servitude was hardly an original scheme. Four of them having changed their names, each claimed to be an only son. The authorities must have winked—perhaps having been bribed to do so—at this sort of very obvious dissembling, because it was so commonly utilized by desperate young men during the middle and late nineteenth century. To the traditional Jews of Eastern Europe, surnames were of little consequence, being used only for legal or other official purposes. At the time young Weinberg transformed himself into young Nuddleman, it had been less than a century since governments began to insist that all citizens have a surname. To Jews, surnames continued to be of far less importance than patronymics—for example, Yitzhak ben Avraham (Isaac, son of Abraham), or Rivkah bas Yaacov (Rebecca, daughter of Jacob). In such an atmosphere, men and women forsook their family names without pangs of conscience, because their family heritage dwelled in other things. In time, I would do the same.

I learned all this Nudelman lore from a few conversations with distant cousins, but I did have just a bit of more personal information. I came by it in later years, through my interpretation of two old photographs among the many more recent ones displayed under the plate-glass top of the bureau in my parents' bedroom. I have not seen either of those pictures in almost forty-five years, but I remember both as though they were lying before me at this moment.

One was of Daddy's entire family, minus him. It was no different from the hundreds of similar portraits I had seen of families in those times and places, except for the appearance of the three teenage boys standing solemnly alongside their older sister, behind their seated middle-aged parents. In the photo, my grandmother Minge and my bearded grandfather

Noach stare without expression into the camera, looking exactly like the old-world Jewish elders that they are. Their plain, slightly plumpish dark-eyed daughter (whose name I never learned) stands to the right, behind her seated father. Alongside are her three younger brothers, who look remarkably like Russian peasant boys. Their short hair, about the length of a crew cut, is light in color and could in fact be blond. Were it not for the company with whom they are seen, there is nothing that might suggest to an observer that they are Jewish.

The other photo was of a staunchly erect young man wearing the belted and strapped parade uniform of a private in the Russian army. His left hand grips a cane, upon which he depends for support, and his leg on that side is held stiffly in front of him, as though he cannot bend it at the knee. The proud soldier's hair is darker than it was in the other photo, and he is strikingly handsome. This is one of the sons shown in the other picture—whose name I never learned—now grown to manhood and recovering from wounds sustained in the Great War. I am guessing this last, because it was not something Daddy told me. He never spoke of any of the people in these two photos, any more than he did of the circumstances of his leaving them. It was tacitly understood that no one would ask him about these things. I was a teenager before I heard the least word of the people in the photograph, and even then only because of the events of World War II. I did not learn any of the young people's names until one of the four, my uncle Avram, somehow traced our address and wrote—in Yiddish, of course—from his home in Buenos Aires, hoping to reestablish contact with the brother he had not seen or heard from in almost half a century. My father did not answer those letters. I never asked if Avram was the young soldier.

Although estranged from his immediate family, Daddy nevertheless found a home with one of his father's brothers upon arriving in America. That uncle had four small children, one of whom, Willie, was destined to play a large and devoted role in Daddy's life and in mine. There was also a close relationship with another uncle who lived in that overcrowded warren of tenements, pushcarts, and disease that has become miraculously transformed into a place of nostalgia by a generation that never knew its privations—the Lower East Side of New York City.

I have little idea of how my father sustained himself in his first

American years, beyond his telling me that he managed to scrape together enough money to buy a candy store and then went broke with it.

"I was a lousy businessman," he would tell me in Yiddish. "Altogether too easy a mark. Here's the kind of thing that used to happen. A woman would come in and ask for a glass of cherry soda, which I would mix up for her. She'd drink more than half of it and then complain, saying, 'You made it too sweet, Meyer,' so I'd fill the glass again with seltzer from the fountain. She'd take another long drink and say, 'You ruined it, Meyer. Now there's no cherry taste anymore.' So I'd squirt in more syrup. Of course, then she'd whine that it was too sweet again, but not till she'd taken another big swig. Again, I'd put in more seltzer. And that's how it went: 'Meyer this and Meyer that, and more syrup and more seltzer, and more seltzer and more syrup, and who knows what else, Meyer'—until Meyer finally lost his shirt from these kinds of things. To tell you the truth, Sheppy, I was just as happy, because I hated dragging those big blocks of ice from the curb into the store at five o'clock every morning."

After a few other failures in small business, Daddy, like so many other Jewish immigrants of the time, finally sought out a job working at a sewing machine in one of the garment industry sweatshops along Seventh Avenue. Over the years, he would be employed in a series of such places, always as an "operator," which meant that he and the others so designated sewed together dresses whose parts had been cut and fashioned by more skilled craftspeople. Each of the shops was ruled over by the Boss, a man considered the natural enemy of the employees and of the International Ladies' Garment Workers' Union, founded to confront him in every possible arena from wages to ventilation. Caricatured in the ILGWU literature and strike posters as demanding, avaricious, and caring not a whit for the welfare of the mostly Jewish and Italian immigrants who toiled in his shop, he fought each improvement that cut into his profits. Every one of the bosses I was ever told about seemed to fit the mold, at least as described by those who labored for him.

In a sense, Daddy had entered the family occupation. One of his uncles, Shoil Nudelman, had done the same, and found himself working next to a pretty blue-eyed blonde from Novaradugk, named Vitsche Lutsky. Shoil was the matchmaker, and the two young people, both in their late twenties, married in 1919. My parents' relationship was one of incomprehensible complexity and inconsistency, and even now I struggle to understand it.

I have no idea whether my parents had a romantic courtship, because I never heard them speak of it in later years, except one day when, at the age of nine, I asked my mother how Daddy had proposed. She smiled shyly in his direction and reminded him that he had done it by saying, "Will you go away with me?" The recollection of it brought a look of sweet gentleness into his eyes, but the moment lasted only a second, as though such warm memories were not to be permitted to intrude on the practical events of life's current realities. In later years, I would learn from relatives that the decision of Meyer and Vitsche to marry soon became the cause of a strong undercurrent of resentment in Momma's family. I never definitively ascertained the source of it, but it was hinted that it arose from Rose's continuing single status, because old-world conventions dictated that she should have married first.

So many families of that time had a maiden aunt living with them that she has become a familiar figure in fiction and memoir, and I presume to put Tante Aya among them. From my earliest recollection of her, she seemed interminably busy. She bustled her chunky little self off each morning to the 183rd Street subway station, took the train to her job in a dressmaking loft in New York's Garment District, and then trudged home each evening just before supper. Rose was part of a small circle of unmarried women friends who went together to the movies, to the Yiddish theater, and occasionally to the Metropolitan Opera. One of them always took us kids to the circus when it made its annual visit to Madison Square Garden.

There was a certain brisk and businesslike femininity about Tante Aya. The years had brought added pounds to a figure that was revealed in the old photos as alluringly curvaceous. She was said to have once been very attractive, when her head of thick, buoyant hair was still blond and her light blue eyes flashed with the fire of spirited youth and a razor-sharp wit. Relatives told tales of rejected suitors and her haughty ways with those who continued to pursue in vain. She was a constant presence in our lives—generous and greathearted and at the same time just a bit tart-tongued and minimally tolerant of childish misbehavior. Tante Aya had the energy of a small, squat dynamo. I would never learn the entire secret of the contempt that she and Bubbeh exuded toward my father, or of the obvious ill will for them that he seemed to go out of his way to demonstrate in return.

Rose had no shortage of shtetl-bred suitors. No matter how faded the photographs of those days, it is obvious that—even measured against her three attractive sisters—she had a remarkably lovely face. Her hair was just a bit blonder and thicker than theirs, her eyes a slightly lighter blue. Without doubt, she was the beauty of the family. But there was a haughty selectiveness in the way she repeatedly rejected the inelegant swains who pursued her. She seemed, I was told by people who knew her in that youthful time, to be figuratively (and sometimes literally, too, I suppose) keeping them at arm's length, letting them know that she was made for better men than they. I am certain that it is not my imagination that detects the merest trace of a pout of independence on the lips of the aloof young woman in the old photographs, nor is it my admiration for her absolute self-sufficiency of later years that convinces me that it can be seen in her eyes even at that early time. She was like her mother in this, undaunted by the buffeting of an oafish world, and intolerant of imperfection in herself or others. Not only did those two proud women not suffer fools gladly; their contempt was overtly made evident to any boor who, in their supercritical estimation, earned it.

The young Meyer Nudelman was hardly a boor, but neither was he a very polished specimen of a rising young immigrant. The problem, as it was described to me decades later, was that Meyer seemed unwilling or perhaps unable to do what was required to improve his station. It seemed to the Lutsky women beyond understanding that a man should fail to make any attempt to better himself. To his bride's family, Meyer was still a greenhorn. But there could have been no complaints about the way Meyer looked. In those days, he was a slim, sturdily built man, whose eyes seemed never to lose that appearance of deep sensitivity with which he viewed the world until the day he died.

In his youth, Meyer Nudelman looked like a proud man, and he was. The inconsistency between that and his inertia in attempting to better himself will always puzzle me. His hair, almost black, was parted on the left and combed toward the side, but it had a way of curling itself into a small Napoleonic wave that fell forward onto his broad, high forehead.

Even after it began its lateral spread in later years, that well-nostriled Jewish nose of his conveyed an image of certitude and strength, especially as it overlooked a determined, finely lipped mouth and a strong chin. Meyer's appearance as a young man gave the impression of self-confidence. Even on his limited budget, he made certain that his clothes fit him perfectly, and he took meticulous care of them. But he was a man who stood alone, and at a distance.

His distance was apparent in all things, even in the way he spoke—especially in the language of this country, in which he never found his way. Many of the words and expressions and pronunciations that peppered his speech were inimitable. They were his alone. The next-door neighbor was "ah naybrid ti me"; the dish served at the end of a meal was "rezoyve." When coming in from a game of stickball, I might be told to "Vosh you doidy fayste"; should I delay, it would be said "dvized," or twice. "Tschikahgy" was a midwestern metropolis, as was "Tsintsineddy," whereas "Sen Frensooskie" looked out on the Pacific Ocean. My father knew about these places, although he neglected to become a "tsititsnerr" of the United States until he had been living here for almost forty years.

Though Daddy never said a word about anything he had left behind in Novoselitz, Momma's family did just the opposite about the environs of their town of origin. As we listened to Momma, Bubbeh, and Rose speak, it sometimes seemed that the golden land was the far-off one that had been left, and not this one to which they had come. Their tales of sweet remembrance about that treasured place nostalgically recalled as *der heym*—"our home"—in Russia were many. Its distant rhythms seemed far less turbulent than those of this thief America, or *America gonef,* as they so often called their new place of residence, because it had robbed them of so much.

🍀 *Surgeon, medical historian, and Yale School of Medicine professor Sherwin B. Nuland is also a prolific author. He is perhaps best known for* How We Die: Reflections on Life's Final Chapter, *which won the 1994 National Book Award. By the time he wrote* Lost in America: A Journey with My Father *(2003), his father had been dead some four decades.*

Nuland was born Shepsel Nudelman in 1930, the youngest of three sons of Meyer and Vitsche Nudelman. The family living in the crowded Bronx apartment also included Vitsche's mother and sister. Bronchial pneumonia killed the eldest son at the age of three; the middle son, Herschel, was disabled by rheumatic fever in his teens; and Vitsche died when Shepsel was only 12, leaving him to care for a father who suffered from mysterious, debilitating physical ailments and towering, unpredictable rages.

Everything about the father was a source of searing embarrassment to the son. Indeed, Nuland is unsparing in relating his youthful cruelties to his father. Yet in 1947, when the Nudelman boys wanted to change their name to something less obviously Jewish, Meyer petitioned the court on their behalf. "I was not proud of the course I was embarking upon," Nuland remembered, but "if I could get away from Nudelman, I could get away from Meyer."

Nuland went on to graduate from the Bronx High School of Science, New York University, and the Yale School of Medicine. Leafing through a medical textbook at Yale, he discovered the cause of his father's symptoms: Meyer had suffered from tertiary syphilis his entire adult life—a fact his doctors knew but never told him. The shocking knowledge led to some easing of the painful father-son relationship, but Meyer died shortly afterward. Although Meyer remains "a constant looming presence in everything I do," in Lost in America *Nuland has begun to make peace with his past and with himself, a peace revealed in his choice of epigraph—words from the Jewish philosopher Philo of Alexandria: "Be kind, for everyone you meet is fighting a great battle."*

Trudier Harris

Summer Snow

My mother was never bitten by a snake, either on a fishing bank or in the fields or woods into which she eagerly waded to wrest new garden space from the wilderness or to shoot a squirrel or rabbit for a hearty stew. I can only surmise that her quickness at snake-killing exceeded the speed of any snake. The most frightening tales she told involved coach whips, those constrictor-type snakes that would wrap around a person and squeeze the breath out of them. She had come across a few and had always managed to beat the devil out of them—again the biblical connection—before they managed to go into their almost always fatal coils. I conclude that my mother was particularly blessed, that her guardian angel, knowing that her children had already lost their father, was keen to keep a shield of safety around her to prevent her early demise from snake bite.

My sister Hazel tells the story of her and her neighbor Mary Stallworth going fishing with Momma on a creekbank near their homes. Mary had been sitting under a big tree fishing for quite a while when she heard a plop above her head. She looked up and saw that a huge snake had fallen from one tree limb to the next lowest one. She yelled for Momma, and the two of them got big sticks and started pushing and pulling at the snake trying to make it come down—so they could kill it. Meanwhile, Hazel says, she just sat on her fishing bucket a safe distance away and watched the drama. Momma and Mary kept after the snake, but they didn't have sticks long enough to force it down. They now recognized it as a coach whip, for it had wrapped itself tightly around the tree and couldn't be dislodged. Then Momma said, "I know what. Let's us pretend that we leaving. It'll come down then." Hazel says she had no idea that Momma was right, but once they packed their gear, gathered their poles, and started away, the snake slithered down. It obviously had not observed that Momma and Mary were still carrying their big sticks. They dropped their poles, advanced on the snake, and started beating it. Momma yelled out for Hazel to help. "That snake ain't done nothing to me, so I ain't gon' bother it," Hazel replied. No such sentiment ever stopped Momma. She and Mary beat the snake to death. When the snake was dead and Momma held it up as high as she could with her stick, both its head and its tail were still touching the ground. That means the snake must have been at least eight feet long. Now, we all laugh when that story is told. I am puzzled, though, as to what led my mother to execute such risky behavior. Perhaps these adventures gave her after-fishing smiles.

For all her snake-fighting adventures, however, my mother was a staid fisherwoman. She could sit on the bank of a river all day, but she would not get into a boat—at least not until Ed finally convinced her to do so when she was well into her seventies. Before then, she would go with her fishing buddies, or one of her children or grandchildren, and sit contentedly waiting for some unsuspecting fish to grace her hook and dinner table. I always call my mother Champion Fisherwoman of Tuscaloosa, Alabama, and over the years I have dedicated books to her using that designation. Momma thought nothing of getting up at three-thirty or four o'clock in the morning, gathering up her fishing supplies and some meager lunch of a honey bun and sardines, and heading to the nearest riverbank until six, seven, or eight o'clock at night. There were times when she would be gone so long that I would begin to worry about her. After all, she couldn't swim either, and who knows when she might have slipped down a riverbank? But she always came home safe and sound, absolutely elated with her catch. She would be so energized from the conversations on the riverbank that it always made me curious about the topics she and her fishing buddies discussed.

Fishing was the site on which Momma exercised clear notions about how to treat one's neighbors (which didn't include snakes). I began giving her driving lessons when she was sixty-three, and the family bought her a car shortly after she earned her driver's license. Now she could drive herself—and offer to drive others—to her favorite fishing holes. So she would be ringing someone's phone in the wee hours of the morning looking for a fishing buddy, or someone would be ringing her phone. For the many years she had driven with other folks, she always contributed to gas costs. When she started driving, she always asserted that it did not take more gas to drive four people in the car than it did to drive one, so she mostly refused to allow her passengers to pay for fishing trips. I say "mostly," because there were a few occasions on which someone prevailed upon her to take a few dollars.

In the later years of my mother's life, fishing was fun—pure and simple. She did not need the fish she caught as a food supplement and would frequently give her catch away to neighbors or other family members. The only thing she required was that they do the cleaning themselves. Catching the fish had been sufficient pleasure for her. The smiles and laughter that would come when she described the pull of bringing in a larger fish or when she recited some venture at the riverbank were memorable. It was the family's duty at that point in her life to keep her in "fishing money." She didn't smoke, drink, or have any other vices. She just loved to fish. She loved the company of the women with whom she fished. She loved the outdoors. And she loved the satisfaction of a good fishing outing. It would keep her in smiles until, well, the next morning, when another fishing buddy called for an outing.

If ever any of her children were planning a surprise for Momma, they could easily effect it once she set off for a riverbank. There would be time to plot surprise birthday parties, which we did for her seventieth birthday, or have her garden tilled, or sneak in any number of other little treats. It was the time to bring in new clothes that someone had bought for her (practically everybody in the family shopped for her and could fit her almost perfectly). During one such fishing outing, one of my brothers bought Momma a new white suit. When she returned and completed her usual after-fishing ritual (cleaning the fish, taking a bath, rubbing down in alcohol to dislodge any little creature that might have thought it had found a home), the new outfit was brought out for Momma to try on. It was absolutely gorgeous and a perfect fit. The story goes that she went next door to my brother Ed's house, pranced in, modeled the outfit, and said: "Give me a Band-Aid, 'cause I'm so sharp I might cut myself." It was a classic ending to a fishing day.

It is perhaps difficult for people outside rural Southern environments to understand the mystique of fishing along riverbanks, lakes, and streams. For the initiated, it is a pleasure that never grows old. For men married to women who are devoted to fishing, they become like football and golf widowers for most of the season that is warm enough to fish. For women like my mother, who were widows, fishing is the engagement that never becomes boring. In the nearly forty years that I was consciously aware of my mother fishing and her attitude toward the sport, I have seen her disappointed only when, for some absolutely unavoidable reason, she could not go. Never did I see her unhappy when she returned from a fishing outing. Instead, those outings energized her the way spinach was portrayed as energizing Popeye. It was like Santa Claus had visited and brought her her heart's desire.

It was most appropriate, then, that on the evening before my mother's homegoing celebration (that is, her funeral), her children, their children, and a host of relatives and friends had a catfish fry. We gathered in the house in which she had lived for twenty-five years and in which my sister Ann now lives. There were probably fifty or so people there. Two of Ann's friends provided the huge electric fryers in which the fish was cooked. Another friend had brought a cafeteria-sized pan of pasta salad. My cousin Joan, who is a cook at a local elementary school, donated huge pans of homemade rolls. French fries and hush puppies were also available, and soft drinks were in abundance.

Although we had just returned from the funeral home, making our final plans for the next day, there was no somberness at this gathering. Everyone there knew that "Miss Unareed," as I had now come to call her, had had a long and wonderful life surrounded by loving children and grandchildren. So we communed over the fish, remembered the woman who had made fishing legendary in our family as well as in her community, and were thankful that on such an occasion as this we could have sustaining, nurturing thoughts. No fishing snake stories emerged that night, but I'm sure at least one was in the minds of several people in attendance.

Fishing takes as much creativity as do the stories that are told about it.

There is a tradition of fishing just as there is a tradition of storytelling about fishing. To be really good at either requires a devotion that most folks give only to their professions. For black folks who fish in Alabama, however, the idea of profession would be anathema to their love of fishing. Though much energy is expended on it, fishing is escape not work. Fishing is what one wants to do, never what one must do. What they bring to the tradition is an undivided love of entering the natural environment of those slippery little opponents and catching them in what they consider a challenging if not exactly fair competition. But then, what has ever been fair about love?

▼ *"I love my first name," writes Trudier Harris in* Summer Snow: Reflections from a Black Daughter of the South *(2003). After explaining how to pronounce it (TRU-dee-uh), she usually has to tell where the name came from. "Because my mother made it up," she says, "each time I explain, I am honoring her."*

The sixth of nine children of Unareed Burton Moore Harris and Terrell Harris, Sr., Trudier Harris was born in 1947 on an 80-acre cotton farm in rural Green County, Alabama. The family was poor, but the farm was nearly self-sufficient: They grew and canned vegetables, and kept horses, cows, hogs, and chickens. When Terrell Harris died in 1954, the family moved to Tuscaloosa.

Unareed urged her children to get an education: "Get something in your head," she would say. "They can't take that away from you." Trudier complied, graduating from Stillman College in 1969 and then earning both her master's degree and her doctorate from Ohio State University. After teaching at the College of William and Mary for six years, she joined the faculty at the University of North Carolina at Chapel Hill in 1979. Widely published in her specialties of African-American literature and folklore, Harris lectures throughout the United States and abroad.

In Summer Snow, *Harris explores her identity as a black woman in the American South. "It took a couple of decades before I realized that my mother was supporting a money-making tradition, not an intellectual one," Harris writes. Indeed, she saw with pain that neighbors and church members shied away from her, intimidated by her professional status. "It has taken me a long time to arrive at a basic fact of my existence: I am a Southerner," Harris writes. "For a Black person to claim the South, to assert kinship with the territory and the mores that most Black folks try to escape, is about as rare as snow falling in Tuscaloosa during dog days. It's a reconciliation that many African Americans have not yet made."*

Sue Miller

The World Below

I magine it: The long, difficult birth. The baby unable to be turned. The mother, finally incapable of any control at all, given over simply to screaming. Then the ether, the cutting, and the rich metallic smell of blood and amniotic fluids. The child, limp, too still and grayish at first, then, with the shock of air, squalling into purple life—a boy, his genitals absurdly swollen, his body slick with matter and blood.

Then his arrival at the party, still wearing his dark work suit, still carrying in his mind the astonishment of the birth, and somehow, he felt, the scent of blood. The wave of voices from within the house, the lovely girl turning to him in a dress the odd color of her own lips as they curved into her mouth, the sudden plunge into talk and laughter and celebration.

And through it all, her face lifting to his over and over, as though she had never truly seen him before. Hello. Hello again. Once they bumped into each other and she turned and said "Oh! It's you!" in a way that made him feel she had been waiting for him forever. For him.

Imagine it: the bachelor approaching middle age, whose need to earn his way through college and then medical school had kept his young life austere and straitened; called to a half-rural practice in Maine, part surgery, part obstetrics, part nearly worthless medicine, part commiseration. He was grateful—and then ashamed of his gratitude—to ether, to morphine, to laudanum. His patients were grateful too, even when he could do virtually nothing for them. "Doc" they had called him, from the time he was less than thirty, and it made him feel old and prematurely sorrowful.

Imagine joining the army, being sent to France—the base hospital— full of a shameful eagerness and sense of adventure (for how could this be his freedom, his liberation, this war that had brought catastrophe to Europe and death to thousands and thousands of boys so much younger, so much less liberated than he?), only to find his first task to be uselessly ministering to the scores dying of influenza, drowning in it as it swept through the confined quarters where they lived together. To feel, even as he began his work over there, how powerless he was to be.

Imagine it: the talismanic memory that comes to him from time to time through all of this, the memory of an early evening in Maine, weighted already, even then, with the sense of what he cannot do, with the growing sense of what medicine itself cannot do, parking his motorcar outside the Rices' home. He is late; this is his last stop before he goes to his own empty house, this stop to give Fanny Rice a shot of morphine that will, perhaps, let her sleep through the night. He dreads it, what she's been reduced to: her greedy, cawing voice, the way she weeps sometimes in relief as the drug releases her. As he gets out of the car, his eye is caught by the sense of motion, by a pale dancing glimmer on the deeply shadowed front porch. Ah! it's the oldest child, Georgia. She's heard his car and come out to greet him. But for a moment, standing there in her blue dress, drying her hands on a dish towel, her long ribbon of hair falling over her shoulder, she looks like a young woman, not a child; and he is struck, having had the image of Fanny in his mind as he reached across in the car for his bag (Fanny: weightless, skeletal, her flesh yellow and dried)—he is struck by her solidity, her mobile, youthful beauty, the sense of a contained vitality in her. His heart lifts as he steps into the shadow of the house—he can help *her* after all, even if he can't help her mother—and it almost seems to him for a moment that the girl, this sturdy, grave child, must have intended this gift to him, must have know how he needed it.

But no, she is just relieved. "I thought you'd never get here!" she cries impatiently.

"But you were wrong, weren't you?" he answers, and his reward is the surprised, wide smile—she likes to be teased—and then the light way her hair and her dress bell away from her as she turns to lead him in.

Georgia: she has already been with him through so much.

He died when I was nineteen, a freshman in college, and my grandmother's grief was surprising and almost frightening to me. She had seemed so well used to his being old, so tough-minded about it, so gently mocking of all his foibles as well as of their long history together, that I thought she had a great distance on everything. I had, in fact, presumed his age to be a kind of burden to her and his death to be expected, even counted on.

I came home for his funeral, all the way across the country from California. The house was crowded. Her children, the two who were still alive, had come home too, Rue from France, my uncle Richard from New York. They took Lawrence's and my bedrooms, and we slept downstairs, he on a cot in my grandfather's office and I on the couch in the front parlor. We all foraged for ourselves at breakfast—my grandmother didn't come down until midmorning. It was this, almost more than anything else, that let me know how acute her sorrow was.

She tried to hide it from us. Three or four times each day, when she felt it overwhelming her, she'd go to her room and close the door. There was never a sound from behind it—I actually listened once, to my shame—but when she emerged, her eyes would be red-rimmed, her voice hoarse, dried out.

The service was in the Congregational church on the green, a memorial service, since he'd been cremated. We walked up slowly, and ahead of us as we turned onto Main Street we could see others, dressed in their somber clothes, walking in the same direction. It was still mud season, and those who had come farthest wore galoshes or boots with their Sunday clothes. The air smelled of wet earth. As we approached the green, we saw the cars lined up, completely surrounding the square, some pulled up onto the grass. They left deep ruts that were slowly filling with water.

The minister was young, new, and it was clear he hadn't known my grandfather well. But he kept his part of the service short. It was an old friend, another retired physician, who delivered the eulogy, which was warm and funny. Then we all sang the familiar songs, my grandmother's thin soprano strong through them, and walked back again to the house for the collation.

The house was full at the start, and it had the feeling of a party, people who hadn't seen each other all winter catching up with one another's news. There was no great shock to my grandfather's death, of course—he was eighty-eight—and that made it easy for people to move quickly from consolation to news and gossip.

After an hour and a half or so, though, we were winnowed down to the family and to about twenty people who'd known my grandparents well. Ada and Fred were both there, sitting on the couch in the back parlor, she looking like a fatter and somehow more smug version of my grandmother—who sat quietly most of the time in her favorite chair, speaking only when someone spoke directly to her. Others in the room had pulled dining room chairs in here as the party thinned, and a few people were standing, holding coffee cups or drinks. Who was it who started the stories—Dr. Butler, who'd taken over my grandfather's practice after he retired? or George Hammond, who fished with him? or Ada, who could tell tales of the early part of her sister's marriage: of the day my grandfather marched Georgia down to the bank and set her up with her own account, for instance—the only woman Ada knew for years and years who could claim to have her own money.

I could have told my own stories too, of course. I could have spoken of my grandfather's funny language for food, designed just to please me, I thought as a child: eggs "done to death," fried potatoes "smashed to smithereens" and doused with "gobbets of gooey gravy."

I could have described how he'd taught me to drive on the dirt road that ran by Miller Pond, calmly and unflappably reading as I fumbled through the gears and stalled out repeatedly, as I lurched to the shoulder or narrowly missed trees; calling out loudly only if the car began to falter or cough, "It's gas what makes the car go, Cath: *gas, gas, gas!*"

During those lessons, we'd sometimes stop and picnic on the promontory where they later built a summer camp for boys. He would open what my grandmother had prepared with an eagerness that seemed to me to transcend hunger—that had to do, I always thought, with the connection he felt to her, through this food she'd made. Afterward, stuffed, I would sunbathe on the old khaki blanket and he would fetch his fishing rod from the trunk of the car and move around the edge of the lake, casting off out beyond the lily pads. Sometimes I watched him, or waded, feeling the sunfish brush my ankles or nibble at my bare feet. And then we'd drive again. I think now he probably had instructions to keep me out of the house all day so my grandmother could reclaim her solitude. Could nap.

I could have described the long letters he wrote to me at college, reminiscing about his own undergraduate days, calling me back to my wavering purpose—the life of the intellect, wasn't it?—by remembering his with such clarity and fondness. Once he wrote:

> There was a secondhand bookstore a few blocks off campus which I used to haunt with friends. You can imagine my pleasure at finding a first edition of Carlyle there one day. I spent almost a full week's wages on it.

I could imagine no such thing, of course, but it made me aware, momentarily, of wishing I were the sort of person who could.

I could have said he was always the one who tended to me when I was sick, arriving at my bedside before I called out for him sometimes, with cold water to drink and cool cloths to wipe my face, my hands and forearms. That he didn't believe in aspirin for a fever unless it got dangerously high. He'd look at the thermometer and shake it down, saying, "Good for you, Cath, you're burning the bugs up."

I didn't say any of this, I think because they felt too dear to me, too private, these memories; and my grandmother said nothing either, perhaps for the same reason.

✣ *In her novel* The World Below, *from which this excerpt is drawn, Sue Miller traces the personal journey of Catherine Hubbard, who inherits the Vermont homestead of her grandmother and discovers her own sense of place when she immerses herself in her grandmother's journals. Like Catherine in her fiction, Miller in fact possesses a number of journals compiled by her own great-great-grandmother, who was a farmer's wife and worked as a milliner in Maine. Largely concerned with daily matters—one entry read, "A fine day. I churned in the morning. John went to Plymouth."—the journals also contained gemlike revelations: Miller came across one that confided, "I'm a person whose every wish is destined to be denied." As Miller put it, "I just wanted in some way to honor those or to use them."*

Born in Chicago in 1943, Miller comes from a family of preachers and academics. Her minister father taught church history at the University of Chicago. Her mother was a poet. At age 16, Miller entered Radcliffe, the women's college at Harvard, and married her first husband shortly after graduating in 1964; her son, Ben, was born in 1968. Miller and her husband divorced three years later.

Suddenly a struggling single mother, Miller took in lodgers and founded the Harvard Yard Child Care Center, where she worked for eight years. During that period she wrote scarcely at all, but the daycare center ultimately proved to be a rich source of material. As she told a British interviewer, "Unlike mathematics, where everything can be over for you if you haven't done your best work in your 20s, writing is rewarded by experience."

The phenomenal success of The Good Mother *(1986), her first novel, allowed Miller to write full-time, punctuated by the occasional teaching stint. She dedicated her sixth novel,* The World Below, *to one of her grandmothers. "She wrote to all of us all our lives," Miller said. "She had 17 or 18 grandchildren and wrote to all of our spouses. As long as she could see and make her fingers work, she wrote letters daily to everyone. And just kept track of all of us for each other. She was really the center and the linchpin of our family's life."*

Ted Kooser

Memory

Spinning up dust and cornshucks
as it crossed the chalky, exhausted fields,
it sucked up into its heart
hot work, cold work, lunch buckets
good horses, bad horses, their names
and the names of mules that were
better or worse than the horses,
then rattled the dented tin sides
of the threshing machine, shook
the manure spreader, cranked
the tractor's crank that broke
the uncle's arm, then swept on
through the windbreak, taking
the treehouse and dirty magazines,
turning its fury on the barn
where cows kicked over buckets
and the gray cat sat for a squirt
of thick milk in its whiskers, crossed
the chicken pen, undid the hook,
plucked a warm brown egg
from the meanest hen, then turned
toward the house, where threshers
were having dinner, peeled back
the roof and the kitchen ceiling,

reached down and snatched up
uncles and cousins, grandma, grandpa,
parents and children one by one,
held them like dolls, looked
long and longingly into their faces,
then set them back in their chairs
with blue and white platters of chicken
and ham and mashed potatoes
still steaming before them, with
boats of gravy and bowls of peas
and three kinds of pie, and suddenly,
with a sound like a sigh, drew up
its crowded, roaring, dusty funnel,
and there at its tip was the nib of a pen.

✴ *The people, places, and things of the Great Plains crowd the plainspoken lines of Ted Kooser's poem "Memory." Lauded as "an oracle of the ordinary," the two-time Poet Laureate of the United States (2004-2006) and winner of numerous poetry prizes and awards writes often about his own memories and the importance of memory to writers.*

Born in Ames, Iowa, in 1939, Kooser earned a B.S. at Iowa State University in 1962 and an M.A. at the University of Nebraska in 1968. In Lincoln, he worked as an insurance underwriter and executive for 35 years before retiring in 1999. The day job is what let him write poetry—between 4:30 and 7:00 every morning before work. When he got to the office, he would deposit his latest creations on his secretary's desk and say, "Does this make any sense to you, Joanne?" If she replied no, Kooser reported, "I would try to find out where it fell down for her."

Kooser lives on an acreage near the town of Garland, Nebraska, with his wife, Kathleen Rutledge, and two dogs. "I've got an armchair down in the living room where I prop a cup of coffee on one arm and set my notebook on my lap… and see what happens," he says. "If you're not there writing, it's never going to happen. My friend Roger Welsch out in Dannebrog, Nebraska, says, 'You got to be there when the geese come flying in,' you know. It's just that sort of a thing."

3 | By Passion Driven

"We are not the same persons this year as last; nor are those we love. It is a happy chance if we, changing, continue to love a changed person."

—W. Somerset Maugham

Robert Bly

A Third Body

A man and a woman sit near each other, and they
    do not long
At this moment to be older, or younger, or born
In any other nation, or any other time, or any other
    place.
They are content to be where they are, talking or
    not talking.
Their breaths together feed someone whom we do
    not know.
The man sees the way his fingers move;
He sees her hands close around a book she hands
    to him.
They obey a third body that they share in common.
They have promised to love that body.
Age may come; parting may come; death will come!
A man and a woman sit near each other;
As they breathe they feed someone we do not know,
Someone we know of, whom we have never seen.

Robert Bly was in his late 40s when he wrote the ethereal love poem "A Third Body" in the mid-1970s, which would not appear in book form for another decade (Loving a Woman in Two Worlds, *1985*).

Probably best known as the founder of the "Iron John" men's movement, Bly also found success as an editor, translator, and speaker. He was born in Madison, Minnesota, in 1926 and enlisted in the Navy at age 18. After a stint at St. Olaf College in his home state, Bly transferred to Harvard in 1947, where he met the poets Adrienne Rich and Donald Hall. He graduated in 1950, then earned an MFA from the University of Iowa Writers' Workshop in 1956.

On a Fulbright grant awarded in 1956, Bly traveled to Norway, where he discovered many poets whose work had not yet appeared widely in English. To introduce such writers as Pablo Neruda, Rumi, and César Vallejo to a larger audience, Bly created the literary magazine The Fifties, *which became* The Sixties *and* The Seventies. *He also co-founded American Writers Against the Vietnam War in 1966 and donated to antiwar causes the prize money that came his way from a 1967 National Book Award for his poetry collection* The Light Around the Body.

In the 1970s, Bly grew intrigued by the ways in which myths and fairy tales define gender roles. Unlike women, he argued, men were ill-equipped to express their emotions. At gatherings, Bly took to recounting the German folktale of a wild old man who aids a young prince. As he explained in Iron John: A Book About Men *(1990), the story helps men mentor one another, and it models positive methods of expressing masculinity.*

Bly penned the introduction to The Best of American Poetry 1999; *in 2006 he agreed to sell his papers to the University of Minnesota.*

Diana Athill

Yesterday Morning

T here was no—or no conscious—physicality in these early loves, yet while they were going I was spending a great deal of time thinking about sex. Indeed, from the age of eleven, when revelation occurred, except when my mind was being positively invaded in one way or another, I thought of little else.

Revelation took the form of a small black book with nothing written on its cover. Why I pulled it out of a book-case's bottom shelf where it was tucked away in a corner, I cannot imagine, but when I had read on its title-page the words "Wise Parenthood" I started to turn the pages, supposing I was about to discover some method of raising children properly that my mother had once hoped to follow. As a result, I was never to suffer what she suffered on her honeymoon. From that early age I knew—not approximately but exactly—what men and women do in bed; and I also knew that it was one of life's best pleasures, and that I was going to start enjoying it *the minute I was old enough.*

The revelatrix was Marie Stopes, that absurd—even monstrous— woman who yet did more for her fellow-women than almost anyone else in the twentieth century. She made contraception acceptable, and on the way there she taught everyone who read her what she taught me. And in my case her lessons were supplemented by a posse of bawdy balladeers who had been collected into six volumes bound in white leather which dwelt in my grandfather's smoking room. Those, too, I fell on by chance.

Every year, either just before or just after the great Spring Cleaning to which her house was always subjected under Hannah's generalship, Gran "did" Gramps's books. His library was extensive and valuable, in her eyes almost sacred, so that no one else was allowed to clean the books, not even Hannah. Gran would put on a cotton overall and one of her sunbonnets to keep the dust out of her beautiful white hair, and every single book she would take out, clap-clap to blow away any dirt settling between the pages, wipe with a soft clean duster, and (if the binding was leather) polish with a special unguent which she kept in a stone jar. She did the library, the morning room and the smoking room, and it took her weeks.

She was halfway through the smoking room when I went in to loll on the sofa and keep her company. The handsome white volumes, which she had piled on the floor near the desk, caught my eye, and I saw the word "Ballads" on their spines. "What are those?" I asked, with what I thought was virtuous curiosity—ballads were supposed to appeal to children because they were usually hearty, but they bored me. "You would-n't be interested in those," said Gran, much too quickly—and in a flash my secret prowler was on to it. That evening, as soon as the house's silence assured me that the grown-ups were safely in the drawing room or the servants' hall, I nipped down and abducted one of the volumes to read under my bedclothes. In those days we didn't use the expression "Wow"—but "WOW" it was.

So I was unusually well-informed for my age, and I found the infor-mation wildly exciting—and yet, being in love was one of the things that served to take my mind off sex. I find it surprising now, but *then* it didn't enter my head that it should be otherwise. Children—because the word "teenagers" was not yet in use, "children" included people a good deal older than it includes now—children did not *do* sex. If a child of thirteen or fourteen dressed or behaved in contradiction of this "fact," I saw them much as I saw someone who dressed or behaved in the wrong way when riding to hounds: absurd, and lacking in taste. When, in my mid-teens, I learnt that someone I actually knew had in fact "done it," I was appalled—so much so that for a day or two I believed I would never recover from the shock; which was an odd reaction considering that what had been done was something I myself had been dreaming of eagerly for—by then—at least five years. (Fortunately my recovery from this shock was very much more rapid than I expected it to be.)

Women much younger than I am, belonging to generations in which love-making between teenagers is taken for granted, sometimes say that they embarked on sex when they did chiefly because it was expected of them: they would have looked silly to their contemporaries if they had been unwilling. Which makes me suppose that my own lack of resentment at having to wait so long to be "old enough" was largely due to there being no peer pressure. If everybody you know, young as well as old, is thinking in the same way, you need to be a strongly dissident person to think differently. And it is possible—even probable—that some part of me was glad to be given so much time.

THE ACCEPTANCE OF A CONSTRAINT which may seem strange to many people nowadays, gained me, in the years between fourteen and eighteen, an intense experience of erotic pleasure, getting nearer and nearer to that of full love-making, which was thoroughly enjoyable. The first time a man's hand closed on mine and I turned mine so that our palms met was so exquisitely exciting that it still stirs me to remember it. Then came the first time someone sitting beside me in the back of a car put an arm round me and pulled me towards him so that my head rested on his shoulder; the first time a man, having done that, brushed my forehead with his lips (urgent question: would be it be cheating to count that as *being kissed?);* the first real kiss, followed by the first open-mouthed kiss; the first hand on a breast, followed by the first unbuttoning leading to hand and lips on a bare breast (a tremendously exciting leap forward, that was)… And so it went on, incident by incident, each one pondered, savoured, dreamt about: the haze of sexy daydreaming through which I floated in those days must have been almost tangible.

It didn't matter much who was doing the touching or kissing, because I had fallen in love when I was fifteen (goodbye, dear David, goodbye!) and was quite sure that it was Paul's bed into which I would eventually sink; but he was five years older than I was and I had to catch up with him before I could expect him to fall in love with me. I was practising… and loving every moment of it.

Dances were where it mostly happened, ranging from modest "hops" in small houses to full-scale balls in big ones, and including going with a group of friends to places such as the Assembly Rooms in Norwich where public dances were held, usually on a Saturday night. Mine was the first generation of country-house girls allowed to go to dances unchaperoned. To begin with we were driven in my grandmother's sedate car (complete with fur rug, footwarmer and speaking-tube) by Mr. Youngman, her chauffeur, who collected us at midnight. The earliest moves in love's game were therefore given an extra thrill by taking place secretly, under that rug. But soon young men with wheels were invited to dinner and drove us to the dances… The true beginning of the sexual revolution for us came long before the sixties, with the car. Once a man and girl who had been dancing together all evening were able to drive home alone together in that little capsule of safe privacy, the deliciously slow progress towards loss of virginity accelerated to a rush.

BEING SENT TO BOARDING-SCHOOL helped to check this rush, as far as I was concerned, and probably for other girls, too (though I gained the impression that I was looking forward to its conclusion more eagerly than most of my friends). School happened to me when I was fourteen, and made freedom part-time. A result of no one's recognizing the teens as a separate condition was impatience to be grown-up: although I no longer felt like a child, I was having to bide my time before bursting forth as what I did feel like, which was more or less adult. Boarding-school was a good way of getting through this not-quite-yet time; it controlled restlessness within a discipline that I could accept because it was part of the set-up as a whole, not directed at me as an individual.

There was one moment, some time in my seventeenth year, when I broke ranks. A particularly good dance was being given by some grand neighbours of ours, not long before the end of my school's winter term. It seemed a pity that I should miss it, so much so that my mother hit on a solution: my teeth did in fact need attention, so she asked my headmistress if she could take me for a day's visit to a London dentist, which would mean keeping me out for a night—and the date of the dentist's appointment (this, of course, was not revealed) was that of the dance, for which we could get back from London just in time. It was a delightfully daring plan: no present-day schoolgirl can have any idea of the convent-like seclusion imposed by headmistresses in my day. Letters were censored, outings apart from those at half-term were forbidden, no girl was ever allowed to leave the school grounds alone, and it didn't occur to anyone that parent and child might communicate by telephone. Permission to visit a London dentist was a favour so great that even by its agonizing self (no injections in those days, except for extractions) it would have been a treat.

Early on the morning after the dance my father drove me back to school, and left a note for the headmistress, with whom he got on well, confessing that I had been to a dance. His almost obsessive honesty compelled him to it, but he certainly didn't feel that he was purging a serious sin: he expected her to find it funny.

Instead, I was summoned to her study and threatened with expulsion. So violently did she berate me that what began as a schoolgirl's dismay at being found out suddenly switched to an adult's astonishment at absurd over-reaction, so that when at last she thundered: "Have you no sense of honour at all?" I answered coldly: *"Not* if that is what you mean by a sense of honour." I can no longer remember how the interview ended, except for having a gratifying sense that she was disconcerted; and she must, when she recovered from her rage, have seen that she was making a mountain out of a molehill. She did, to my father's amusement, write him a pompous little note telling him that he had not behaved like a gentleman, but she did not expel me—indeed, I ended as the school's head girl. The incident remained in my mind as a pleasing one—the tip of a toe in the sea of being grown-up.

The daughter of an army officer and his wife, Diana Athill was born in 1917 and educated at home in Norfolk, England, until she was 14 by governesses she has described as "very amiable and amateurish." After boarding school, she went on to read English at Lady Margaret Hall, Oxford, graduating in 1939.

During World War II she worked for the BBC, and in 1943 she had a brief affair with André Deutsch, which concluded amicably. When Deutsch started his first publishing firm shortly after the war, Athill joined him as editor, continuing in that position until her retirement in 1993 at age 75.

At André Deutsch, Athill edited the likes of Norman Mailer, John Updike, Margaret Atwood, and V. S. Naipaul. But the writer whose approach she most sought to emulate in her own work was Jean Rhys. "She had very simple rules about writing," Athill once said. "You must get it right; you mustn't waste an unnecessary word."

Athill's several memoirs are acclaimed for their insight, wit, and a rare gift for seeing unpleasant truths about herself. Whatever happens to her, she has often said, a "beady-eyed watcher" is always present. Some have noted that the rawness of her memoirs can make them painful reading. Athill's response: "There is no point in writing from personal experience unless you try to be as honest as you can… I write to get to the bottom of things."

In Instead of a Letter *(1963), Athill describes without self-pity how, as a young woman, her fiancé had jilted her after a two-year silence, sending a formal note asking to be released from their engagement. The blow was enormous: Despite her career success, Athill felt a dismal failure for decades. But the writing was cathartic. "I wrote that book and I got completely rid of that feeling," she told an interviewer. "It was extraordinary. It's like starting a new life. And I've never felt like that again since."*

Gioconda Belli

The Country Under My Skin

I don't remember what came first—poetry or conspiracy. All my memories from that period are luminous, close-up images. Poetry was the result of that exuberant, life-giving spirit. Once I could assert my power and strength as a woman I felt able to shake the impotence our dictatorship made me feel, with all the misery it had sown. I could no longer believe that change was impossible. I had reached a boiling point, and my body celebrated this wonderful affirmation. The simple act of breathing was a thrill. I drank the world in, and I was possessed by such a feeling of plenitude that I wondered how my skin could contain me. Any day now, happiness, like an ectoplasm, was going to spill out of my pores, and I would float off, naked, dancing through the streets of Managua.

One day I walked into the Poet's office, and saw him with a lanky, wiry young man with a face like Don Quixote. He had teeny eyes hidden behind giant eyeglasses, and a long, thin mustache.

"Camilo Ortega," the Poet said to me. "Sit. Camilo just told me that they almost took him away yesterday."

"So," Camilo said, continuing his story as I sat down. "They were about to throw me in the back of their jeep, so I shouted as loud as I could. 'I'm Camilo Ortega and they're taking me away!' You know—the worst thing is for them to get you without anyone else knowing about it. So I yelled and yelled. People came out of their houses. The soldiers got nervous. They hadn't counted on my screaming like that. One of them walked over to me, kicked me from behind and then pushed me around—not to force me into the jeep, just to kick me out of the way and get rid of his urge to beat me up. Then they got in the jeep and drove off."

"And your brother? How is he?"

"It's hopeless. They're not letting him go. In December we'll stage a protest. We'll do graffiti, take over a church, the usual. 'Christmas without political prisoners.'"

"Daniel is Camilo's brother. He's one of the Sandinistas in jail," the Poet explained to me.

I wondered if Camilo was a Sandinista too. He seemed different from the artists and dilettantes I knew. He was quiet but intense, as if he were concentrating hard on something, and he had an air of responsibility that made him seem far older than his years. He spoke softly, almost in a whisper. But what I noticed right away was the intangible power he held over the Poet, who now seemed placated and serious—something highly unusual for him. He gave Camilo a copy of *Praxis,* the magazine he edited, which served as a forum for the group of artists, writers, and painters who worked together under the same name. We discussed the magazine: the essay by Ricardo Morales Avilés about the responsibility of the intellectual, the recently debuted Praxis gallery, which held recitals and art exhibitions. We talked about the widespread anger at the recent price increases—transportation, milk, and bread had all just gone up. Before he left Camilo asked us if we had seen the movie *Woodstock.* The music was great, he said. Joe Cocker did a fantastic rendition of the Beatles song "With a Little Help from My Friends." And then there was Jimi Hendrix and his guitar. We had to see it.

Camilo came back to the office a few more times. We would go across the street to a juice stand where you could look out toward the Gran Hotel, the tropical hotel par excellence in those days, with a green awning and an entrance hall filled with palm trees and birdcages with parrots and macaws. The sidewalks, littered with potholes and loose bricks, bristled with activity—throngs of people bustling about, traffic jams in the streets, taxis honking like mad, as well as a few horse-driven carriages. Modernization had hit Managua like a steamroller, transforming the city into a crazy hybrid of tradition and progress.

CAMILO ASKED ME to join the Sandinistas. By then, I was pretty familiar with all the signs and symbols of the underground movement. In the artsy circles, the Sandinistas were regarded with admiration and respect. I had now read all the books I needed to convince me that armed struggle and revolution were Nicaragua's only chance. George Politzer's book, *The Fundamental Principles of Philosophy*, turned me into a philosophical materialist; Frantz Fanon, in *The Wretched of the Earth*, gave me a crash course in colonialism, neocolonialism, and the realities of the Third World. Eduardo Galeano, in *Open Veins of Latin America*, revealed to me the sad, bloody history of my part of the world, and taught me about Big Stick politics, the Alliance for Progress, and the loathsome consequences of the Monroe Doctrine, which declared that "America was for the Americans"—meaning that the American continent had to be considered the exclusive backyard of the United States. I had also read Marcuse, Chomsky, Ernst Fisher, and Che. Socialism had won me over. But joining the Sandinistas was a risky proposition. It meant putting my life in the line of fire. I had my doubts too: the theory known as the "guerrilla focus" had worked only in Cuba. And what kind of system were they proposing, exactly? The Soviet model, from my point of view, placed far too many restrictions on personal freedoms. And how would we foment a revolution without a proletariat? Camilo, who didn't have a car, would often ask me to drop him off at the university on my way home. During the ride, he'd lecture me on subjects ranging from the failed military tactics of the guerrilla focus to the ideology sponsored by Sandinismo. The revolution would not be communist, he'd say, but Sandinista, which meant that it would incorporate various theories, including Marxism, but adapting them to our specific reality. He had an answer for everything, and boundless reserves of patience to respond to my many doubts.

When he asked me whether I was ready to join the Sandinistas, to give him a straight yes or no answer, I confessed that fear prevented me from committing myself.

"All of us are afraid. That's normal."

"But I have a daughter…"

He didn't ask me to go underground. I could do little things. Nothing risky, but enough to make my own contribution.

"Your daughter is precisely the reason you *should* do it," he said. "You should do it for her, so that she won't have to do the job you are not willing to do."

He was right. I couldn't choose to be a coward.

"All right," I said quickly, without flinching, thinking of the way one slips under a cold shower.

"Don't tell anyone," he said. "Not a word. Not even to the Poet. This has to be between you and me. It's a question of compartmentalizing, of minimizing the risks."

IT WAS NIGHT by the time we reached the university, a series of simple, prefab structures connected by hallways and staircases, protected from the elements by corrugated tin roofs. I dropped him off at the parking lot, and watched him disappear into the corridors. My stomach churned as I drove toward my house. I passed through slums, I saw the dilapidated buses slow down to pick up the passengers who piled in, hanging off the doors even as the bus heaved onward. Somewhere within my anguish, a sudden sense of relief—maybe it was joy— washed over me. It was as if the guilt of privilege had suddenly been lifted from my shoulders. I was no longer another transient observer, contemplating the misery from the comfort of my car. I was now one of the people fighting it. I cared about how the people of Managua were suffering, day in and day out, and I would prove it by doing something to effect a change. And that made me feel less alone, for a reassuring voice inside me lifted my spirits and calmed my fears. I was so relieved to leave behind that paternalistic Christian-style charity that always brought me back to the convent school nuns who, each Christmas, asked us to bring gifts for the girls of lesser means who attended our school in a separate annex next door. According to the rules, all gifts had to be the same: a piece of fabric, candy, and a toy. When it was time to give them out, the nuns would line us up in pairs, one rich girl and one poor girl. One by one, in front of the Mother Superior, the gifts would be handed over. As I waited my turn in line, the heavy, shapeless present, wrapped by my mother in simple, plain paper, felt like such an obvious welfare package. I always felt so terrible for the other girl—for her, the ceremony must have seemed like a well-intentioned form of humiliation. Troubled by the role I was forced to play, I could barely look at her as I handed over the gift. Then, we would kiss each other on the cheek and go to the end of our respective lines. That was the only time of year we ever laid eyes on each other, and that was what charity meant to me.

But this was different. I was on the other side now.

At home, everything was the same. Caught up in his work and his depression, my husband barely noticed me. We did some things together, but of our daily life the things I remember most are his apathy, his lethargic gestures, and the television screen, like the glow of a life he could look at but never really touch or feel. I fulfilled my role as wife and mother, and played with Maryam in the garden amid the abundant foliage. Thoughts and verses would spring up in my mind like kernels of popcorn frying in the hot oil of my secret life. It occurred to me that the words were banging down my door, begging to be written down, yet I resisted committing them to paper. Somehow I felt as if the act of writing would ruin the charm and the emotion of the images I conjured up in my head. I was better off staying where I was, standing motionless by my daughter's swing, watching her romp around while words and phrases rolled before my eyes as if written on banners floating in the sky.

I described all this to the Poet.

"Write," he said. "Write about what you feel. You have a responsibility—a historic one." His eyes were intense, serious.

The next day I arrived at the office with six poems. Shyly, I placed them on his desk.

"I wrote them last night," I said. "They just came out, like rabbits."

He took the sheaf of papers. He lit a cigarette. He sat back in his chair. He propped his feet up on his desk. The Poet had a potbelly from all the rum and beer he loved to drink. He wore long-sleeved shirts. As he read the poems, he exhaled long curls of cigarette smoke.

"Very good," he said, as he went from one page to the next. His voice, deep and clear, sounded surprised. Years later he would confess how astonished he had been by what I, a relative novice, had written— he had been half joking when he made that "historical responsibility" comment. He finished reading, stood up, and walked around the desk to sit down next to me. I can't remember his exact words, but something in his voice told me that he meant what he said. That was when Carlitos Alemán Ocampo arrived. The Poet gave him my poems to read, and Carlos seconded his opinion.

"They need a little work," said the Poet. "Once you get to be like us"—he allowed himself a devilish grin at that—"all your writing will be grand, but in the beginning you have to polish, edit. A poem should be like a tamale, closed up and tightly bound. Nothing extraneous, but nothing missing either. Take a look at this one, for example. Study it. Think about the words it doesn't need."

"I'm sure you can get Pablo to publish them," Carlitos said. "He'll love them."

I worked hard as I weighed each word, removing myself so that I could look at the poem objectively, without me in the middle. It was so hard. That lovely metaphor, for example, was unnecessary. I marked it. I was never able to be a very merciless surgeon, because I was so infatuated with words. Only with time has it become easier.

We went in to see Pablo Antonio Cuadra, the editor of *La Prensa's* literary supplement. He had a proud bearing, like a Nahuatl prince. His dark skin was the color of cinnamon and his thicket of hair, pure white. He was a tall man, with an elongated body that could have walked right out of an El Greco painting. I felt as if I were in the presence of a living monument, for this was Nicaragua's most renowned poet. His office was packed with books, folders, papers. Just outside sat his chubby, long-haired, moon-faced secretary who pecked away frantically at her typewriter. Rosario Murillo. I would get to know her later on.

"I'd like to publish these poems. With a portrait of you next to them," said Pablo Antonio. "When would you be free for a sitting?"

Not long after, Róger Pérez de la Rocha arrived at my house to paint my portrait, which he did in black printer's ink. We ended up having a lot of fun. Even my husband laughed, watching us like someone studying exotic animals in an encyclopedia. Róger was another character from Managua's bohemian scene—a jovial young artist like all of us. He cursed nonstop and hummed ranchera music as he worked. He was a barrio kid, proudly so, but extremely well read, able to recite from memory entire poems by Carlos Martínez Rivas.

Barely fifteen days after I had written my first poems, *La Prensa Literaria* published them, devoting almost an entire page to me. "A new voice in Nicaraguan poetry," read the headline next to the portrait Róger had painted. I looked dark and mysterious.

"YOUR POOR HUSBAND," one of my aunts commented the day after the poems appeared. "How could you write—and publish—those poems? What on earth would make you write about menstruation? How awful. How embarrassing."

"Embarrassing?" I retorted. "Why should I be embarrassed?"

My aunt looked at me, horrified. And with an *ay! hijita!*, she got up and left.

THE PUBLICATION OF MY POEMS was nothing less than a scandal which rocked the upper echelons of Managuan society.

"Vaginal poetry," declared the matrons. "Shameless pornography."

"It's a good thing you published them under your maiden name," remarked my mother-in-law. Men leered at me with hungry, knowing looks.

"You must be quite a passionate woman," they would say with glazed eyes.

It was 1970. I wasn't saying anything that had not been said before by men, but I was a woman. It was not done. Women were objects, not subjects of their own sex drive. I wrote joyfully about my body, my passion, my pleasure. The poems were not explicit—they weren't even remotely pornographic. They were simply a female celebration of her senses, the wonder of her body. But they created an uproar.

My husband then announced to me that he didn't want me

publishing any more poems unless he read and edited them first. Absolutely not, I told him. Over my dead body. I would give up writing first. Fortunately the High Priests of Nicaraguan literature rallied to my defense. The great poets José Coronel, Pablo Antonio Cuadra, and Carlos Martínez Rivas championed my cause. And in Nicaragua, poets are venerated, celebrated figures. Our national hero, the most acclaimed Nicaraguan, is Rubén Darío, a poet who is considered the Father of Modernism in the Spanish language. To be known as a poet in my country is to enjoy one of the highest, most cherished status symbols in society. My husband and family, finally, were forced to surrender to the blessings of prestige.

The controversy didn't deter me—it inspired me. To upset the most conservative circles of Nicaraguan society made me realize there were more ways than one to subvert the establishment.

The Poet, meanwhile, was busy building fabulous castles in the air, fantasies in which he and I would live happily ever after, writing poems to each other on our naked bodies until the end of time. My love for him, though, was more like that of a playmate, a partner in crime. The Poet would have been a nightmare as a husband. I could never picture him sharing responsibilities—he would have dumped them all on me as he went on proclaiming his "wild exuberance."

It wasn't long before I realized that when you break certain societal rules there is always a price to pay. The rumors grew louder and louder, until they eventually reached my father's ears. Blissfully ignorant in the happy little bubble we had created for ourselves, the Poet and I acted as though we were invisible. Instead of treating one another as furtive lovers, we walked through the city streets smelling of sex, our hair tousled and our eyes aflame. Anyone could see that we were euphoric, possessed by both the passion and defiance we liked to think only a chosen few ever knew. Unfettered in our arrogant sense of freedom, we made love on mattresses surrounded by canvases and smelling of turpentine in the tiny, ramshackle studios of our artist friends or in borrowed apartments. We even made love on top of our desks at work, giggling as papers went flying in every direction, gasping for breath to muffle the sounds of our lovemaking as typewriters hummed and coworkers bustled about outside our office door. Our cheeky disregard for discretion made us the hot topic of local gossip. Even my absent, distracted husband began to sit up and take notice. Sooner or later someone was going to say something to him. There was no way on earth I could escape the obvious: I had to make a decision: stay with the Poet—and assume the corresponding risks—or return to the familiarity of my marriage. No matter what I chose, I knew that nothing would ever be the same. I had grown wings. I felt ready to take flight. But the Poet was like a hurricane, too turbulent for me to handle, and I was terrified at the prospect of making the wrong decision and dragging my daughter with me. When I saw how my father was suffering, I made up my mind.

I'll never forget the look on the Poet's face on the other side of the desk when I told him. I feel as though I can still see the landscape behind the window, hear the rumble of the air conditioner. We couldn't go on like this, I said. I couldn't go with him. He had figured as much, he said. He knew it would have been too hard on me, having to confront my entire family about it. The conversation was sad, but not tragic—I think we both understood that we had pushed things as far as they could go. At least we still had our friendship, our mutual affection. More than anything I felt relieved—I was worn out by the tension of the weeks that had led up to this, and all the subterfuge that went with it. And while the Poet may have sparked the revolution that now raged inside me, I knew that what I felt went far beyond him or any partner I would ever have.

"I would have made you happy," he said, wrapping his hands around mine.

"You *did* make me happy," I replied.

He smiled. He was never one for melodrama. He got what he could out of life but he also knew when to give in.

NOT LONG AFTERWARD, I changed jobs, sometime in the middle of 1972, I think. I was really making an effort to extricate myself from that love affair, like a snake shedding a layer of skin. I returned to the regular, married life I had been sleepwalking through during my affair. It was a shock to see my husband again as the man who shared my life, my bed, the morning bathroom rituals, when for many months I had dismissed him from my life. The payoff was slim: sure, I didn't have to worry about accusations—"I know you have a lover"—and I suppose I felt honorable again. In spite of myself, I was mortified by the malicious smiles of my mother's friends, as they elbowed one another whenever I walked by, and the men who would cluster around me murmuring all sorts of double entendres as if I were wearing some sort of sign inviting them to try their luck with me. Much later on I would stop caring about what they said, and even relish disturbing their hypocritical sense of decency. But I hadn't quite reached that point yet. At the time, my fear of ostracism, of being left out in the cold, won over the need I felt to get away, to leave that environment altogether.

Camilo Ortega was the person who helped me realize it was important to keep up the pretense of my bourgeois life. The more time I spent undercover, without raising any suspicion, the more useful I could be to the Sandinista movement. By maintaining a facade of innocence and continuing to do my rounds in the traditional social circles, I could keep my finger on the pulse of the bourgeoisie, and report their feelings and thoughts regarding the dictatorship. Being an upper-class woman was an ideal alibi for my subversive endeavors. I knew that I had to keep my position in that world in order to eventually blow it up from the inside.

Not long afterward, Camilo told me he was going away for a long while. Someone else would call me, he said, and through that person we would resume contact. We said goodbye on a street corner.

That was the last time I saw him.

Gioconda Belli believes that the course of her life was determined on the day she was born in 1948, when her mother, pregnant with the future writer, went into labor while attending a baseball game at stadium in Managua, Nicaragua. In the taxi en route to the hospital, they passed a statue of Nicaraguan dictator Anastasio Somoza, whose strongman son would be overthrown in the 1970s.

As a result, she writes in her autobiography, The Country Under My Skin, *she has always been drawn to the warmth of crowds. Instead of becoming "a bat-wielding athlete," she became a revolutionary, "taking up arms against the descendants of that horse-riding despot" and performing "heroic exploits between changing diapers and boiling baby bottles."*

The mother of four children from three marriages, Belli also managed a trio of impressive and interlocking careers: as an advertising executive, as a diplomat in the Sandinista administration, and as an acclaimed poet and novelist.

A member of Nicaragua's upper classes, she attended a school for advertising and journalism in Philadelphia in the mid-1960s, then returned home to work for the Alfa Omega Ad Agency, among others. Her advertising career came to an abrupt halt when the younger Somoza's chief of security alerted her employer to Belli's burgeoning political activism. Though shadowed by the Nicaraguan secret police, she smuggled weapons to the leftist Sandinista revolutionaries before the 1979 revolution that brought down Somoza.

Belli's transition to director of public relations and communications under the new Sandinista government began when she co-wrote the first issue of a revolutionary newspaper and flew back to her homeland from Costa Rica with a planeload of freshly printed copies. Her literary career blossomed on a parallel track with her political activities.

Belli now lives in Santa Monica.

Elmore Leonard

When the Women Come Out to Dance

It was hot down in this scrub pasture, a place to wither and die. Ruben Vega loosened the new willow-root straw that did not yet conform to his head, though he had shaped the brim to curve down on one side and rise slightly on the other so that the brim slanted down across the vision of his left eye. He held on his lap a nearly flat cardboard box that bore the name L. S. Weiss Mercantile Store.

The woman gazed up at him, shading her eyes with one hand. Finally she said, "You look different."

"The beard began to itch," Ruben Vega said, making no mention of the patches of gray he had studied in the hotel-room mirror. "So I shaved it off." He rubbed a hand over his jaw and smoothed down the tips of his mustache that was still full and seemed to cover his mouth. When he stepped down from the bay and approached the woman standing by the stick-fence corral, she looked off into the distance and back again.

She said, "You shouldn't be here."

Ruben Vega said, "Your husband doesn't want nobody to look at you. Is that it?" He held the store box, waiting for her to answer. "He has a big house with trees and the San Pedro River in his yard. Why doesn't he hide you there?"

She looked off again and said, "If they find you here, they'll shoot you."

"They," Ruben Vega said. "The ones who watch you bathe? Work for your husband and keep more than a close eye on you, and you'd like to hit them with something, wipe the grins from their faces."

"You better leave," the woman said.

The blue lines on her face were like claw marks, though not as wide as fingers: indelible lines of dye etched into her flesh with a cactus needle, the color worn and faded but still vivid against her skin, the blue matching her eyes.

He stepped close to her, raised his hand to her face, and touched the markings gently with the tips of his fingers, feeling nothing. He raised his eyes to hers. She was staring at him. He said, "You're in there, aren't you? Behind these little bars. They don't seem like much. Not enough to hold you."

She said nothing, but seemed to be waiting.

He said to her, "You should brush your hair. Brush it every day...."

"Why?" the woman said.

"To feel good. You need to wear a dress. A little parasol to match."

"I'm asking you to leave," the woman said. But didn't move from his hand, with its yellowed, stained nails, that was like a fist made of old leather.

"I'll tell you something if I can," Ruben Vega said. "I know women all my life, all kinds of women in the way they look and dress, the way they adorn themselves according to custom. Women are always a wonder to me. When I'm not with a woman I think of them as all the same because I'm thinking of one thing. You understand?"

"Put a sack over their head," the woman said.

"Well, I'm not thinking of what she looks like then, when I'm out in the mountains or somewhere," Ruben Vega said. "That part of her doesn't matter. But when I'm *with* the women, ah, then I realize how they are all different. You say, of course. This isn't a revelation to you. But maybe it is when you think about it some more."

The woman's eyes changed, turned cold. "You want to go to bed with me? Is that what you're saying, why you bring a gift?"

He looked at her with disappointment, an expression of weariness. But then he dropped the store box and took her to him gently, placing his hands on her shoulders, feeling her small bones in his grasp as he brought her in against him and his arms went around her.

He said, "You're gonna die here. Dry up and blow away."

She said, "Please..." Her voice hushed against him.

"They wanted only to mark your chin," Ruben Vega said, "in the custom of those people. But you wanted your own marks, didn't you? *Your* marks, not like anyone else... Well, you got them." After a moment he said to her, very quietly, "Tell me what you want."

The hushed voice close to him said, "I don't know."

He said, "Think about it and remember something. There is no one else in the world like you."

HE REINED THE BAY to move out and saw the dust trail rising out of the old pasture, three riders coming, and heard the woman say, "I told you. Now it's too late."

A man on a claybank and two young riders eating his dust, finally separating to come in abreast, reined to a walk as they reached the pump and the irrigation ditch. The woman, walking from the corral to the house, said to them, "What do you want? I don't need anything, Mr. Bonnet."

So this would be the Circle-Eye foreman on the claybank. The man ignored her, his gaze holding on Ruben Vega with a solemn expression, showing he was going to be dead serious. A chew formed a lump in his jaw. He wore army suspenders and sleeve garters, his shirt buttoned up at the neck. As old as you are, Ruben Vega thought, a man who likes a tight feel of security and is serious about his business.

Bonnet said to him finally, "You made a mistake."

"I don't know the rules," Ruben Vega said.

"She told you to leave her be. That's the only rule there is. But you bought yourself a dandy new hat and come back here."

"That's some hat," one of the young riders said. This one held a single-shot Springfield across his pommel. The foreman, Bonnet, turned in his saddle and said something to the other rider, who unhitched his rope and began shaking out a loop, hanging it nearly to the ground.

It's a show, Ruben Vega thought. He said to Bonnet, "I was leaving."

Bonnet said, "Yes, indeed, you are. On the off end of a rope. We're gonna drag you so you'll know the ground and never cross this land again."

The rider with the Springfield said, "Gimme your hat, mister, so's you don't get it dirty.'

At this point Ruben Vega nudged his bay and began moving in on the foreman, who straightened, looking back at the roper, and said, "Well, tie on to him."

But Ruben Vega was close to the foreman now, the bay taller than the claybank, and would move the claybank if the man on his back told him to. Ruben Vega watched the foreman's eyes moving and knew the roper was coming around behind him. Now the foreman turned his head to spit and let go a stream that spattered the hardpack close to the bay's forelegs.

"Stand still," Bonnet said, "and we'll get her done easy. Or you can run and get snubbed out of your chair. Either way."

Ruben Vega was thinking that he could drink with this ramrod and they'd tell each other stories until they were drunk. The man had thought it would be easy: chase off a Mexican gunnysacker who'd come sniffing the boss's wife. A kid who was good with a rope and another one who could shoot cans off the fence with an old Springfield should be enough.

Ruben Vega said to Bonnet, "Do you know who I am?"

"Tell us," Bonnet said, "so we'll know what the cat drug in and we drug out."

And Ruben Vega said, because he had no choice, "I hear the rope in the air, the one with the rifle is dead. Then you. Then the roper."

His words drew silence because there was nothing more to be said. In the moments that Ruben Vega and the one named Bonnet stared at each other, the woman came out to them holding a revolver, an old Navy Colt, which she raised and laid the barrel against the muzzle of the foreman's claybank.

She said, "Leave now, Mr. Bonnet, or you'll walk nine miles to shade."

There was no argument, little discussion, a few grumbling words. The Tonto woman was still Mrs. Isham. Bonnet rode away with his young hands and a new silence came over the yard.

Ruben Vega said, "He believes you'd shoot his horse."

The woman said, "He believes I'd cut steaks, and eat it too. It's how I'm seen after twelve years of that other life."

Ruben Vega began to smile. The woman looked at him and in a few moments she began to smile with him. She shook her head then, but continued to smile. He said to her, "You could have a good time if you want to."

She said, "How, scaring people?"

He said, "If you feel like it." He said, "Get the present I brought you and open it."

He came back for her the next day in a Concord buggy, wearing his new willow-root straw and a cutaway coat over his revolvers, the coat he'd rented at a funeral parlor. Mrs. Isham wore the pale blue-and-white lace-trimmed dress he'd bought at Weiss's store, sat primly on the bustle, and held the parasol against the afternoon sun all the way to Benson, ten miles, and up the main street to the Charles Crooker Hotel where the drummers and cattlemen and railroad men sitting in their front-porch rockers stared and stared.

They walked past the manager and into the dining room before Ruben Vega removed his hat and pointed to the table he liked, one against the wall between two windows. The waitress in her starched uniform was wide-eyed taking them over and getting them seated. It was early and the dining room was not half filled.

"The place for a quiet dinner," Ruben Vega said. "You see how quiet it is?"

"Everybody's looking at me," Sarah Isham said to the menu in front of her.

Ruben Vega said, "I thought they were looking at me. All right, soon they'll be used to it."

She glanced up and said, "People are leaving."

He said, "That's what you do when you finish eating, you leave."

She looked at him, staring, and said, "Who are you?"

"I told you."

"Only your name."

"You want me to tell you the truth, why I came here?"

"Please."

"To steal some of your husband's cattle."

She began to smile and he smiled. She began to laugh and he laughed, looking openly at the people looking at them, but not bothered by them.

Of course they'd look. How could they help it? A Mexican rider and a woman with blue stripes on her face sitting at a table in the hotel dining room, laughing. He said, "Do you like fish? I know your Indian brothers didn't serve you none. It's against their religion. Some things are for religion, as you know, and some things are against it. We spend all our lives learning customs. Then they change them. I'll tell you something else if you promise not to be angry or point your pistol at me. Something else I could do the rest of my life. I could look at you and touch you and love you."

Her hand moved across the linen tablecloth to his with the cracked, yellowed nails and took hold of it, clutched it.

She said, "You're going to leave."

He said, "When it's time."

She said, "I know you. I don't know anyone else."

He said, "You're the loveliest woman I've ever met. And the strongest. Are you ready? I think the man coming now is your husband."

It seemed strange to Ruben Vega that the man stood looking at him and not at his wife. The man seemed not too old for her, as he had expected, but too self-important. A man with a very serious demeanor, as though his business had failed or someone in his family had passed away. The man's wife was still clutching the hand with the gnarled fingers. Maybe that was it. Ruben Vega was going to lift her hand from his, but then thought, Why? He said as pleasantly as he was able, "Yes, can I help you?"

Mr. Isham said, "You have one minute to mount up and ride out of town."

"Why don't you sit down," Ruben Vega said, "have a glass of wine with us?" He paused and said, "I'll introduce you to your wife."

Sarah Isham laughed; not loud but with a warmth to it and Ruben Vega had to look at her and smile. It seemed all right to release her hand now. As he did he said, "Do you know this gentleman?"

"I'm not sure I've had the pleasure," Sarah Isham said. "Why does he stand there?"

"I don't know," Ruben Vega said. "He seems worried about something."

"I've warned you," Mr. Isham said. "You can walk out or be dragged out."

Ruben Vega said, "He has something about wanting to drag people.

Why is that?" And again heard Sarah's laugh, a giggle now that she covered with her hand. Then she looked up at her husband, her face with its blue tribal lines raised to the soft light of the dining room.

She said, "John, look at me.... Won't you please sit with us?"

Now it was as if the man had to make a moral decision, first consult his conscience, then consider the manner in which he would pull the chair out—the center of attention. When finally he was seated, upright on the chair and somewhat away from the table, Ruben Vega thought, All that to sit down. He felt sorry for the man now, because the man was not the kind who could say what he felt.

Sarah said, "John, can you look at me?"

He said, "Of course I can."

"Then do it. I'm right here."

"We'll talk later," her husband said.

She said, "When? Is there a visitor's day?"

"You'll be coming to the house, soon."

"You mean to see it?"

"To live there."

She looked at Ruben Vega with just the trace of a smile, a sad one. Then said to her husband, "I don't know if I want to. I don't know you. So I don't know if I want to be married to you. Can you understand that?"

Ruben Vega was nodding as she spoke. He could understand it. He heard the man say, "But we *are* married. I have an obligation to you and I respect it. Don't I provide for you?"

Sarah said, "Oh, my God—" and looked at Ruben Vega. "Did you hear that? He provides for me." She smiled again, not able to hide it, while her husband began to frown, confused.

"He's a generous man," Ruben Vega said, pushing up from the table. He saw her smile fade, though something warm remained in her eyes. "I'm sorry. I have to leave. I'm going on a trip tonight, south, and first I have to pick up a few things." He moved around the table to take one of her hands in his, not caring what the husband thought. He said, "You'll do all right, whatever you decide. Just keep in mind there's no one else in the world like you."

She said, "I can always charge admission. Do you think ten cents a look is too high?"

"At least that," Ruben Vega said. "But you'll think of something better."

He left her there in the dining room of the Charles Crooker Hotel in Benson, Arizona—maybe to see her again sometime, maybe not—and went out with a good conscience to take some of her husband's cattle.

✱ *Spare but telling dialogue is a hallmark of Elmore Leonard's 41 novels and numerous short stories. As is clear in this excerpt from the story "Tonto Woman," he is also adept at conveying, as one reviewer put it, "the often parallel exchanges of men and women as they connect and miss connections… he hears what women say, and—much rarer—he also hears what they hear."*

Born in New Orleans in 1925, Leonard was raised in Detroit, where he still lives with his wife, Christine. Following a stint in the Seabees during World War II, he graduated from the University of Detroit in 1950 with a degree in English and found work as an advertising copywriter.

By writing for two hours before work, he churned out 30 pulp westerns and five western novels from 1951 to 1961. Two of his stories, "3:10 to Yuma" and "The Tall T," were made into movies, as was his novel Hombre, *which starred a young Paul Newman. In the 1960s, Leonard switched from westerns to crime novels with the publication of* The Big Bounce *(1969).*

"My main characters, my male leads, really don't have high aspirations," Leonard says. "They are content, that is, happy with themselves, and I find this in my own work. If I don't try so hard, it works better. Yogi Berra said you can't think and hit at the same time."

As for women, Leonard has been married three times. During the first marriage, he told an interviewer in 2005, he had a love affair, got divorced, and married his lover, Joan. When she died in 1993, "I felt I had to get married again. Quickly," he said. "I like being married. Just then, the French-speaking landscaper showed up." Christine was 24 years younger. "We started talking and that was it," Leonard said. "I remember saying to a friend, 'I'm thinking of marriage again, but Joan's been dead for only six months. Don't you think I should wait a year?' He said, 'What are you, Sicilian?'"

Dagoberto Gilb

Gritos

That December was a mist against the skin at six-fifteen a.m., a slimy dew that burned away only hours after the sun rose. I switched on the wipers; squealing, a few streaks. It was almost too cold to have the car window down on the drive to the job site. I wore a sweatshirt until, an hour with the hammer and nail bags, concrete mud and rock, I was warm enough, and then the gray winter shadow of moisture in the air became another of afternoon smog. Winter wasn't cold but an absence of hot, a T-shirt. Winter in Los Angeles is grayer than in spring and summer and fall.

It was Saturday, a half-day of OT, tools back in the lockup, and before I headed home, I drank a few of the beers with the crew next to the superintendent's shack by the excavation pit, a city block big, off 2nd and Beaudry. It would be called a clear day in Los Angeles, the sky would be called blue. Three months earlier we'd moved into a two-bedroom apartment in East Hollywood. We'd left the last apartment, which was cheaper, because of a little legal disagreement with the land-lord. I'd had this job—a thirty-story poured-in-place—for two months, and if I didn't get laid off, it would last a year or more. As depicted by an artist on a billboard next to the site, it was the first of a projected four highrises to go up against the Harbor Freeway.

Once I got home, I wasn't even able to think of a shower before Becky slammed through the door.

"Come on!" she told me. "We have to go now!" She was holding the baby, Ricardo, in her arms.

"What?"

"He called me a stupid Mexican." As black as her hair was, her eyes glared even blacker. "I am so mad!"

"What?"

"This man. When I was pulling out, he didn't like something I did, and so he screamed at me. 'You stupid fucking Mexican! Why don't you learn to drive?' I almost had an accident driving back. You just had to be there, I had to get you."

She was furious. She did have this primordial temper—ancient, pre-Columbian. When we had fights, we really had fights. I imagined them as telenovela metaphors of the conquest, a spilling of Indian and Spanish blood.

"He's not getting away with it," she said. "I wish I were a man. He thinks he can say that to me, I can't believe he thinks he can get away with saying that to me."

"So where's Toño?" I asked. He was five.

"He's waiting for us in the car."

I shook my head as a kind of sigh of resignation: there was no back-ing off. It had been years since she'd made any demand like this. The first time, not long after we met, she escorted me to a telephone booth, where she'd been waiting so patiently, where some rude guy refused to get off the phone. She told me once, Why have a boyfriend who's big if he can't do what I always wish I could?

It wasn't a long drive, a few blocks away, off Vermont and Santa Monica.

"He might not be there by now," I suggested. I was still having to work myself up some, getting mad, too, but I had converted, decided she was right. Seemed like we were getting a lot of this stuff lately. Like whenever we walked into the store owned by those Armenians around the corner, they'd watch us—all Mexicans were thieves, you know.

"He went into the restaurant. I saw."

"But you probably only know him by the car he drives."

"I'll recognize him."

We parked in the mini-mall lot. It was where the nearest Laundromat was, where a bakery that sold the best buñuelos and pan dulce was. She led our family into the House of Pancakes, ignored the sign about letting the hostess do the seating, and up the first aisle, Ricardo pressed against her shoulder with one arm, holding Toño's hand with her free one, until she stopped.

"Him," she said.

It was a booth by the window, a parking-lot view. I centered myself on the open side of the Formica table, directly across from the salt and pepper, the sugar and diet creamers, and the flavored syrups. He was seated at my left, my age give or take, a much older man across from him. Stunned, the two of them had absolutely nothing to say, even though their mouths seemed to be reacting.

"You remember her?" I said. "You called her a stupid fucking Mexican." I was dirty, concrete dust all over me. My hands were callused and chapped, a weave of wood splinters and tie-wire scratches and scabs. "You remember when you called her that, don't you?" My voice was not soft, even in normal conversation. "You were in your car. You were thinking you were a big man."

"This is not the right place for this," the old man said to me. He looked very scared.

"I'm not talking to you," I said.

"Dad," my guy said. He looked worried beneath my gaze. No, he was definitely not in a very good position, even if he was inclined to respond physically. "Please, Dad."

I was examining his face. His teeth, his nose. I angled just enough toward him, my shoulders squared, my work boots planted. I was right-handed, he was seated on my left.

"What do you want?" he asked.

"What do I want?" I took seconds. Becky was smiling, fierce pleasure, at the guy. Toño had pulled her hand a step behind her and, as though noth-ing unusual was taking place, was staring innocently at something else. I turned my head that direction and saw the waitress standing maybe five feet away, at her chin a tray with plates of eggs and pancakes, a hamburger and fries. She'd been caught midstep, her lips fixed into a zero of alarm.

"I want you to fucking apologize is what I want you to do! I want you to *apologize* to my wife."

His brain was lagging behind the shock.

"You think I'm fucking around? You think I'm not *serious?*"

"He didn't mean it," his dad said. "It wasn't anything. This isn't right."

"Not right?" That was loud.

"Dad," the guy said.

"You are going to apologize!" I was too loud. I was mad, really angry.

"I'm sorry," he said in a quiet voice, almost inaudibly. He was speak-ing to his left hand, which was squeezing his right thumb.

I didn't quibble about quality. "Okay. So you *remember* this next time. You remember."

I led the way out, moving fast because I was worked up but also because I expected to see a cop's uniform and I wanted to avoid that. The restaurant's baby blue and orange decor seemed freshly painted, as cheery as plastic flowers. There wasn't so much as a tang of a fork against a plate. All the eyes were wide and unblinking on us as we circled around that waitress, around the hostess now standing next to her sign, and through the double glass doors and back out into the parking lot.

I was still mad. Mad about everything, mad at her. "So what the hell were you doing here, anyway?" I was backing the car up, and it was the first thing I'd said since the restaurant.

Now Becky was scared of me, too, and her voice turned fragile. "I wanted to buy a Christmas tree," she said. At the corner, a lot had been formed, fenced in by fraying twine. XMAS TREES, $19.95 AND UP. "I didn't know which one you'd like, and I couldn't decide."

Dagoberto Gilb was born in Los Angeles in 1950 to a Mexican mother and a father of German descent. "That's the future of this country," says Gilb of the mixed heritage that so profoundly influences his writing. "This kind of mestizaje *is what we have, the culture we're creating." After attending junior college in Los Angeles, Gilb enrolled at the University of California at Santa Barbara, where he graduated in 1973 with a degree in philosophy. In 1976 he earned a master's degree in religious studies. Soon after that he moved to El Paso, Texas, where he found work as a union carpenter and began writing about his experiences.*

For 16 years Gilb made his living on construction sites, shuttling between El Paso and Los Angeles, all the while contributing stories to small presses and local magazines. National critical acclaim finally came with the publication of his first collection of short fiction, The Magic of Blood *(1993), for which Gilb received the PEN/ Hemingway Award. His novel* The Last Known Address of Mickey Acuna *(1994) was a New York Times Notable Book of the Year.*

Gilb continued to garner praise for his penetrating, provocative glimpses into the psyche of working-class Chicanos in Woodcuts of Women *(2001) and in* Gritos *(2003), his first nonfiction collection. About the latter, the* El Paso Times *wrote: "The reader will discover a Chicano fighting for his place in American literature, a Chicano fighting for respect for the working poor, and even a Chicano struggling against himself, and his worst instincts."*

Richard Russo

The Whore's Child

B ack home in Ithaca, they had made gentle fun of the language of the inn's brochure, in which "resplendent" appeared three times. But Snow had insisted it was perfect for them, suspecting that despite their easy mockery, June secretly had her heart set on just such a place as the Captain Clement precisely for its "meticulously preserved, graceful formalities," its "artful blending of American and English, eighteenth- and nineteenth-century antiques," its "finishing touches of crystal and porcelain appointments," its "romantic ambience and elegant grandeur."

And after all, it was thanks to him that their return to the island, so often discussed, had kept getting postponed for well over a decade. Twice they'd canceled their reservations to accommodate some academic conference—most recently just last Christmas when Snow let himself be talked into his least favorite conference so he could sit on the committee interviewing shortlist candidates for his own position. He should have known better, of course, though he never would've imagined his colleagues might hire, over his strenuous objections, a young fool whose academic specialty wasn't even literature at all, but rather, as he proudly proclaimed, "culture." In the interview he used all the latest critical jargon, and assured the puzzled committee that his research was strictly "cutting edge." A month later, when the boy visited the campus—he seemed no more than twenty, though his vita stated thirty—he'd shown no deference to the department's senior scholars and exhibited a smirking contempt for Snow's own books. That so many of the professor's colleagues remained so enthralled suggested to Snow that perhaps they secretly shared his dubious opinion of his life's work. This realization was so bitter that he'd behaved badly, wondering at the question-and-answer session following the young man's presentation (on "Gender Otherness and Othering") whether students could apply his courses toward their foreign-language requirement.

But the boy was hired and Snow retired, willingly enough when all was said and done. The young fool would get his. In no time he'd be a tenured, fully vested *old* fool, by which time Snow himself would be contentedly cold and dead. Until then, however, he had to face June, who certainly understood that with retirement Snow had no excuses left. The Captain Clement beckoned, and he assured her that they'd enjoy traversing "floorboards worn to a glowing patina by two centuries of perpetual footsteps."

THE MORNING AFTER their arrival, the Snows slept in and went down for a late breakfast in the small dining room. Already seated were the two couples they'd met the afternoon before at tea, the people whose arrival from Newport had been awaited so anxiously by Mrs. Childress. They had mingled rather uncomfortably for an hour or so, the gathering supervised by their host, who seemed intent on holding it together by sheer force of will and a tray of sticky pastries. Later, at a restaurant close by, when the Snows casually mentioned where they were staying, they'd learned something about the Childress woman's anxiety from a loose-talking bartender. The Childresses had bought the Captain Clement only three years before, evidently paying well over two million dollars. "You got any idea how many rooms you gotta rent to pay *that* back?" the bartender had asked, arching an eyebrow significantly. No sooner had they closed on the deal than the bottom fell out of the island's real estate market—not to mention their marriage—and now the woman was good and stuck. The hurricane ruining the last month of the summer season would be the final nail in her coffin. The bartender had explained all this confidently, and without visible empathy.

Indeed, the Captain Clement had an air of abandonment, the Newport foursome being the only other guests. Major Robbins, who owned the yacht, was retired military, and Snow couldn't decide whether he was naturally loud or compensating for deafness. Having been misinformed about the professor's area of study, Robbins had quickly cornered him and announced that he himself was something of a Civil War buff, proceeding to regale Snow with the tactical details of some obscure battle. Snow, loath to offend, first feigned interest, then distraction and finally—when the major said, "Now here's where it gets complicated"—intellectual exhaustion. Robbins was not alone in appearing disappointed when the Snows made their excuses and escaped through the garden, the major's party watching their retreat with the weary expression of people who'd been promised, then cheated of, a lengthy reprieve.

This morning, at breakfast, Robbins's companions looked haggard, as though a single night's sleep had not been sufficient for them to face this new day, though the major himself looked fresh and ready for anything. All four were dressed in beach attire and Snow noted with relief that they had finished eating and were unlikely to invite the Snows to join them. June, who professed to have enjoyed their company, was veering sociably toward their table until Snow touched her elbow and guided her to a table on the other side of the dining room. "Try the Mexican eggs," Major Robbins bellowed.

"I will," Snow promised, holding June's chair for her, a gesture that seemed appropriate here at the Captain Clement.

Mrs. Childress, who had been in the kitchen, came out to greet them and to inquire how they'd slept. Snow had slept badly, but insisted otherwise.

"What a shame we can't offer you breakfast in the garden," the Childress woman said, sounding almost stricken. "But the bees have claimed it, I fear."

From where they sat, the Snows could see that the garden was indeed set up for dining, pristine white tables scattered among the potted plants and hedges. They could also see bees swarming beyond the French doors.

"Are they the price of such lovely flowers?" June wondered.

"Alas, no," Mrs. Childress said, her faintly British accent kicking in again. "It's the storm. The bees are disoriented, or so we're told. They think it's spring."

Major Robbins noisily pushed back his chair. "The beach!" he cried, as if commencing a dangerous amphibious assault, though his troops looked potentially mutinous. The major's wife, the first to venture outside, let out a whoop as the bees closed in and then she bolted for the white trellised arch, arms flying about her head, her companions close behind, also beating the air wildly.

The Snows' waitress was a pretty girl named Jennifer whose tan was dark and remarkably even, Snow noticed when she bent to pick up a fork she'd managed to drop to the floor. He wondered whether it was the girl's clumsiness or her immodesty, given the scoop-necked uniform that caused Mrs. Childress to roll her eyes at June before disappearing into the kitchen.

"South Shore has the best beaches," the girl explained in response to Snow's question about where they might spend the afternoon. "Really awesome bodysurfing."

As the girl said this, he thought he saw a trace of doubt flicker across her heretofore untroubled features, perhaps registering her realization that bodysurfing might not be what these particular guests had in mind.

"Oak Bluffs is nice too," she added hastily. "That's got a lagoon."

Another flicker of doubt—had she insulted them?—and a weak smile, as if to concede she wasn't the person to ask. She didn't know what older people did, or where they did it, or why.

Her plight was so touching that Snow decided to help her off the hook. "Which is the beach with the cliffs?" he asked, suddenly recalling it from their previous trip.

"Gay Head, you mean?" the girl said, surprised. "That's clothing optional."

"Oh," June said with a wry smile. "Well, *that's* out then."

"Right," the girl said sympathetically, though Snow couldn't tell if she was reluctant to shed her clothing in public now or if she was looking ahead thirty years. Actually, if they stayed right around the area where the trail joined the beach, they'd be fine. It was only farther down the beach, beneath the bluff, where the nudists gathered. They liked to

cover their bodies with moist clay from the cliffs—"it's primo skin conditioner"—and then let it dry in the sun. "And don't worry about the
name. Some people think it's a gay beach, but it's not," she concluded,
as if she felt it her duty to allay their fears on this score at least. "They
probably ought to call it something else."

"Perhaps they could call it Primo Beach," June said wryly when the
girl stepped away.

WHILE SHE WAS IN the bathroom changing into the new bathing suit
she'd bought on impulse the day before while they were waiting for the
ferry, Snow called his old colleague, David Loudener, whom they'd
planned to visit in Manhattan on their way back to Ithaca. David was
one of the very few people who knew the details of what had happened
when June suffered her breakdown. In fact, he'd been with Snow when
the police had called to say she'd been found at a nearby shopping mall,
staring into the empty display window of a vacant store, and together
they'd gathered her up and taken her home. Apparently, the only consequence of her brief disappearance was that she'd given her wedding
ring to a stranger.

This was years ago, but "How's June doing?" was David's first question, and Snow imagined he heard concern, perhaps even fear, in his old
friend's voice. Snow again was reminded of his suspicion at the time that
David had blamed him, at least in part, for what had befallen his wife.
"You're going to have to be careful of her," he'd told Snow after she was
released from the hospital, and something in his friend's voice suggested that he doubted that caring for June was a task he was suited for.

"We're both fine," Snow now said, aware that June was probably able
to hear the conversation through the bathroom door. "Anxious to see
you and Elaine." And once again he took down the complicated directions he'd need to follow into Manhattan.

"This is way too young, isn't it," June said when she emerged from
the bathroom, modeling the new white swimsuit.

Snow couldn't tell whether this was true or if it was his wife's posture
that proclaimed, almost defiantly, her determination to act her age. June
was still trim—athletic-looking, in fact—but clearly she was not about
to cut herself any slack. In a sunny mood when she'd gone into the bath-

room, she now appeared discouraged and uncertain. "You look wonderful," he assured her. "Come here."

She ignored this invitation. "It's cut too high in the leg," she said, tracing the line of the suit with her index fingers.

"It's the way they're wearing them," Snow said, though now that she'd drawn his attention to it, he saw what she meant.

"It's the way twenty-year-olds are wearing them," she said. "Twenty-year-olds with primo bodies."

"You look lovely, June."

"You'd let me go out in public looking like a fool, wouldn't you," she said.

"Dear God,"

"At least I had sense enough to buy this," she said, slipping a mesh cover-up over the suit.

As THEY DROVE UP-ISLAND, the devastation of the hurricane became even more pronounced. Obviously, cleanup had been prioritized, and the less populated side of the island was still awaiting attention. Along the winding road, branches and other windblown debris still littered the roadway, though larger downed limbs had been dragged onto the shoulder. The air was thick with yellow bees, which pinged angrily off their windshield.

But further on the landscape opened up, rewarding them every quarter mile or so with a glimpse of blue ocean, until finally the road climbed and narrowed and there was blue sky and ocean on both sides. June's spirits seemed to lift as the car climbed the final stretch toward the lighthouse perched on a cliff. Halfway down the boardwalk path to the beach, they stopped so June could pull off the cotton cover-up, and she surrendered a grudging smile. "There," she said. "Are you happy now?"

"I *was* happy," he protested. "I *am* happy."

"Feel that breeze," she said.

By the time they got to the beach, Snow realized he was out of shape and allowed June to carry the beach chairs while he shouldered the bag that contained their towels and suntan lotion, his wallet, her purse. She didn't even point out that she'd cautioned him against taking these particular chairs—bulky and old-fashioned, with heavy wooden frames—instead of the lighter aluminum ones. These had looked flimsy and chintzy to Snow, who'd thought they should recline in good sturdy beach chairs and sleep in an elegant inn.

At the end of the boardwalk, the beach was relatively crowded with bathers, but by trekking a bit farther they could have a stretch of sand more or less to themselves. "By all means," June agreed. "In this suit I want to be as far away from people as I can get."

It looked to be about three hundred yards to the rocky point, with the red clay cliffs rising gently along the way. They'd gone not quite a third of the way when June dropped their chairs in the sand and said, "This is as far as I go, buddy boy. Look up and you'll see why."

Snow, more tired than he cared to admit, had been slogging through the sand with his head down. "What?" he said.

Further up the beach, directly beneath the tallest cliffs, was another smaller cluster of bathers, which caused him to wonder if there'd been a different path that led more directly down to the beach.

"Those people are naked," his wife said.

Snow squinted, salty perspiration stinging his eyes. "Are you certain?" While recognizably human, the figures down the beach were too far away to be, as his replacement might put it, "gender specific."

"You need glasses," June told him, setting up her chair.

He dropped their bag in the sand. "I need *binoculars.*"

Overheated, they went for a swim. The September water was still wonderfully warm, and Snow, who as a young man had loved to swim, dove into the surf and swam out beyond the breaking waves where he did a leisurely crawl before letting the surf bear him back in. June was not the sort of woman who plunged right into anything, much less the Atlantic, and he was not surprised to see that she was still feeling her way out. She had always been a graceful woman, and now, in her mid-fifties, still had a way of meeting the swells that seemed to him the very essence of womanhood. The waves never broke over her, never knocked her back. Rather, at the last moment, she rose with the water, right up to the crest, and then went gently down again. How long, he tried to recall, since they had made love?

Perhaps his wife was thinking the same thing, because as he swam toward her, her smile in greeting contained not a single reservation, though its cause may have been merely the joy of water, the thrill of buoyancy. "Oh, this is grand," she said, water beading in her hair and lashes. When they embraced, she whispered urgently into his ear, "I'm sorry I've been such a pill."

Such a pill. As Snow embraced his wife, it occurred to him that the last time she'd used this phrase, she'd been a young woman, and their love for each other had been so effortless that whatever had momentarily come between them could be effectively banished with this benign phrase. What it conveyed now was not just a sudden and powerful resurgence of affection and trust, but also promise that the difficulties of their marriage over the last decade might even now be swept aside by a mutual act of will. They could be their old, younger selves again. They would be in love.

Later, as they stood in the warm sand toweling themselves dry, June looked down at herself and said, "Thank heavens it's just us." The bathing suit that when dry had caused her so much anxiety proved, now that it was wet, somewhat less than opaque, and her nipples showed through clearly, as did the dark triangle of her pubic hair. And to Snow's surprise she seemed less upset than she'd been when she emerged from their bathroom at the Captain Clement, insisting that the suit was too young, that she looked foolish.

"Let's move our chairs up under the bank," she suggested with a mischievous glint in her eye, a thing he hadn't witnessed in a long, long while.

"Why?"

But she was already carting a chair and the beach bag toward the bank. Tired, happy and suspicious, he folded up the remaining chair and followed. The tides had eroded the cliffs irregularly, of course, and the spot where June set up her chair was semiprivate. Still, he was astonished when his wife peeled off her bathing suit and stood naked before him, this woman who for years had changed into her nightgown in the bathroom. "Well?" she said.

"Well what?"

"Let me know if we have company," June said, settling into her chair and putting on sunglasses. "Unless you're embarrassed, that is."

"Why should I be embarrassed?" he said, staring down at her.

"Good," she smiled, taking a book out of the bag.

Snow set up his chair next to hers, realizing that a challenge had been issued and there was nothing to do but answer it. When he dropped his bathing trunks, she looked at him critically over the rim of her sunglasses. "I *beg* your pardon," she said.

🌐 *Richard Russo has been called "the most important writer about 'Main Street, U.S.A.' since Sherwood Anderson and Sinclair Lewis."*

He was born in 1949 and grew up in the small town of Gloversville, New York. Pursuing a Ph.D. in American literature at the University of Arizona, Russo realized he would much rather write fiction than academic nonfiction. He finished his degree, but also his first (unpublished) novel—which he harshly describes as "not aborted soon enough." A teacher pointed out to him that it was "written with the eye of a tourist." From that moment on, Russo stuck to what he knows: small towns and the "ordinary" people who populate them. "My forte," Russo says, "is turning out characters that are somehow beneath the radar… because they're not terribly dramatic people necessarily or successful in the ways that we like to measure success, yet you see in their everyday lives a kind of heroism."

Supporting himself and his family by teaching college English, Russo wrote Mohawk *(1986) and* The Risk Pool *(1988). With each novel, he gained more admirers of his wry storytelling ability. After the success of* Nobody's Fool *(1993) and its 1994 film adaptation—on which he collaborated with screenwriter-director Robert Benson—Russo retired from teaching and threw himself into writing full-time, "getting the work done, no matter what happens" by hewing to an established routine.* Straight Man *appeared in 1997. It was followed by* Empire Falls *in 2001, for which Russo won the 2002 Pulitzer Prize for fiction.*

While working on the screenplay for Nobody's Fool, *Russo was seduced by the fast-paced nature of screenwriting (months compared with the years he spends on a novel) and discovered that his gift for dialogue made him especially well suited to the task. Since then, he has written or co-written multiple screen- and teleplays, including adaptations of* Empire Falls *(2005) and* The Risk Pool *(2008). Yet Russo considers himself a novelist first and foremost—despite the 2002 publication of his first collection of short stories,* The Whore's Child, *from which this selection is drawn. His novel* Bridge of Sighs *was slated for release in fall 2007.*

Stanley Kunitz

Touch Me

Summer is late, my heart.
Words plucked out of the air
some forty years ago
when I was wild with love
and torn almost in two
scatter like leaves this night
of whistling wind and rain.
It is my heart that's late,
it is my song that's flown.
Outdoors all afternoon
under a gunmetal sky
staking my garden down,
I kneeled to the crickets trilling
underfoot as if about
to burst from their crusty shells;
and like a child again
marveled to hear so clear
and brave a music pour
from such a small machine.
What makes the engine go?
Desire, desire, desire.
The longing for the dance

stirs in the buried life.
One season only,
                    and it's done.
So let the battered old willow
thrash against the windowpanes
and the house timbers creak.
Darling, do you remember
the man you married? Touch me,
remind me who I am.

❖ *Grief and loss recur constantly in the poetry of Stanley Kunitz, who was born in Worcester, Massachusetts, in 1905 and lived well into his 101st year. His father committed suicide a few weeks before Stanley's birth, precipitating the failure of the family business; his stepfather died when Kunitz was 14, and his sisters died young. Thus the potent imagery of the absent father in his most famous poem, "Father and Son."*

A brilliant young man who grew to love poetry in high school, Kunitz graduated summa cum laude *from Harvard in 1926. He received a master's degree the next year and was planning to stay on as a teaching assistant. Bigotry came to his rescue. "I was told indirectly through the head of the English Department that Anglo-Saxons would resent being taught English by a Jew," Kunitz revealed in a 1974 interview. "It seemed such a cruel and wanton rejection to me that I turned away from academic life completely."*

Working as an editor for the Wilson Library Bulletin, *Kunitz submitted poems to various magazines and published his first collection,* Intellectual Things, *in 1930. It drew virtually no notice. During World War II, he registered as a conscientious objector but was nonetheless required to serve. While he was fighting in Europe his second collection,* Passport to the War, *was published. It too failed to stir the critics.*

Kunitz finally did join academia after the War, accepting a position at Bennington College in Vermont; he went on to teach at Yale, Princeton, and Columbia. "It's stultifying for young poets to leap immediately into the academic life," Kunitz once said. "They would be better off tasting the rigors of a less regulated existence. I was over 40 when I began to teach, and I am grateful now for the difficult years of my preparation."

His intensely vivid, increasingly autobiographical poetry finally caught fire with the establishment in 1958, when his Selected Poems, 1928-1958 *won the Pulitzer Prize. He also garnered the National Book Award for 1995's* Passing Through: The Later Poems, New and Selected, *and was named Poet Laureate of the United States in 2000.*

4 | *Turning Points*

"And then the knowledge comes

to me that I have space within me for

a second, timeless, larger life."

—Rainer Maria Rilke

Derek Walcott

Love After Love

The time will come
When, with elation,
You will greet yourself arriving
A your own door, in your own mirror,
And each will smile at the other's welcome,

And say, sit here, Eat.
You will love again the stranger who was your self.
Give wine. Give bread. Give back your heart
To itself, to the stranger who has loved you

All your life, whom you ignored
For another, who knows you by heart.
Take down the love letters from the bookshelf,

The photographs, the desperate notes,
Peel your image from the mirror.
Sit. Feast on your life.

❋   *Critics have acclaimed poet Derek Walcott as a master of "texture and sensibility," of "lovely detail" and "allusive possibilities." Of mixed African and English ancestry, Walcott was born in 1930 and grew up under British colonial rule on St. Lucia, an island in the Lesser Antilles. He began writing in high school, then self-published his first volume of poetry at age 18. After college, Walcott moved to Trinidad, where he ran a theater company and wrote plays and poetry.*

Much of Walcott's work explores the notion of identity in the Caribbean, a corner of the world that has been subjected to the influence of multiple cultures in language, race, faith, and politics. He achieved international success with his poetry collection In a Green Night *in 1962.* Dream on Monkey Mountain, *widely considered his best play, was published in 1967. Several more dramas and volumes of poetry—notably* Sea Grapes *(1976) and* The Arkansas Testament *(1987)—followed before the appearance of* Omeros *in 1990, which can naively be described as* The Iliad *and* The Odyssey *set in the Caribbean with Caribbean characters stepping into the roles of the famous protagonists. When the Swedish Academy awarded Walcott the 1992 Nobel Prize for literature, it singled out this epic poem as "a work of incomparable ambitiousness."*

Now in his 70s, Walcott teaches creative writing at Boston University and continues to write. His Selected Poems *appeared in 2007.*

Verlyn Klinkenborg

The Rural Life

In 1969 my father and I drove from Sacramento, California, to George, Iowa, to gather a few of my grandmother's belongings. She had lived at the edge of George in a house of dark woodwork, scented by geraniums standing in the winter windows and by a slightly scorched odor from an old electric stove. When my grandfather died, much of the substance seemed to go out of that house, and my grandmother followed him into the earth soon after. Now all that was left were empty cupboards and closets and drawers. We took home to California a stiff wooden chair and an old rolltop desk that had stood in a small room on the second floor, its drawers stuffed with valueless yen brought back by one of my uncles from the postwar occupation of Japan.

For most of their adult lives, my grandparents lived and worked on a farm northwest of George. My father grew up there, and it was unclear what he felt when we came to visit it, as we often did when we still lived in Iowa. I still feel a kinship to that farm—to the house and grove and a long-since reordered pattern of fields—without ever pretending that my feelings could serve as a sort of levy on the place. I suspect my father felt the same way. There wasn't enough land in the family for every one of his father's children to inherit a farm of their own. Besides, this was America, the Midwest, where the idea of a legacy in land only a couple of generations under the plow seemed almost czarist. Instead of farming, my father became a public-school music teacher, a career that appeared to lead away from the soil. In 1966, when he was thirty-nine, he moved west from Iowa with his young family and started again, as many Iowans did, in California.

A few years later Dad bought thirteen acres in the oak and madrone hills east of Sacramento, within sight of the Sierra Nevada, and my brother and sisters and I came home for part of the summer of 1978 to help build a house there. The foundation slab—a rectangular pool of concrete that looked like slick water on an overcast day—had already been poured when I arrived from New York. It was notched into an eastern slope overlooking a ryegrass pasture studded with ponderosa pines. And that's where an old conversation with my father resumed—how expansive that slab seemed, how perfectly level, how smoothly finished, and what it promised about the house we would build upon it with our own hands. Plumb and level and square—while we worked our talk realigned itself around those perfectly unambiguous standards. As subjects go, plumb and level and square sound too rectilinear, but not in the mouths of a father and son looking for something to say. "Close enough"—both of us eyeing a spirit level laid against a beam or along a header—became words of genuine, unexpected complicity.

There had been years of do-it-yourself construction in our household, years of work with drill and hammer, shovel and saw, day after day when I might have spoken this particular language with my dad. When I was a young boy he taught me how to nail together beehive frames and brood boxes in the basement of our house, which he and his brother-in-law built. There was always a project of some kind under way—turning a garage into a bedroom, pouring a new patch of concrete, reroofing the house. But by the time we moved to Sacramento and I entered high school, I was already living on some dark planet orbiting between my ears, inaccessible to the humble claims of amateur carpentry. And no wonder. When Dad got up from the dinner table, disgusted beyond words with another of my ironic impieties, he usually retreated to the woodshop he had built near an apricot tree in the far backyard. Silence and glum looks fell all around the table whenever that happened—until from the shop, rising high above the sounds of traffic on Watt Avenue, came the repeated, inarticulate scream of a table saw. I used to joke that Dad was crosscutting two-by-fours and pretending that each piece of pine was my stiff, impenitent neck. Only my mother found it hard to laugh.

One after another these images gather—crossing the high plains of Wyoming more than thirty years ago during the long drive "back," as we always said, to Iowa, both of us watching the moonlight on the snow between Rawlins and Laramie—the two of us wandering, not quite together, through my grandmother's empty house in George that bitter cold Easter—the sullen distance between us as I drifted into private insurrection in high school and college—and then a picture of him standing between the studs of a wall we had just raised on that new foundation, while behind him, well off to the east, rose the granite peaks of the Sierra Nevada, all their difficulty smoothed by distance.

Now, so many years later, I find myself in a new relation to the old story. I'm as old as my father was when the shape my young life was taking must have looked most hopeless to him, when he might have given up guessing altogether the shape my life would take. Lindy and I have no children, and when the state of our childlessness occurs to me, as it often does, I also think of something my brother John said when his son, Jake, was born—that he suddenly understood Dad in an entirely new way. Instead of a child to understand my father by, I have an old house and this land—a pasture, stone walls, outcroppings of bedrock, and ordinary, acidic soil set in a largely graceless climate. Every time I walk out onto this property with a tool or a pair of gloves or a purpose, I think of my dad walking out, in exactly the same manner, onto his property in the foothills of California. I realize that I've been caught up in an urge—an atavism really—that reaches well past the limits of my own nature. I've discovered a stirring, restless desire to improve this place—to father myself upon it.

My plan in buying this small farm wasn't to tutor the pasture and the sugar maples and the hemlocks. I hoped instead to let the landscape tutor me, to lie fallow for a while myself. But most days I find myself walking out the mudroom door in old jeans and a torn jacket and leather gloves. There are asparagus crowns to be trenched or apple trees or roses to be planted or a garden plot to be tilled. An entire pasture needs refencing. The chain saw needs sharpening, and when that's done there's a pile of logs to be cut into stove lengths. One of the yard hydrants leaks, and the barn needs to be emptied, cleaned, redivided, rewired, hay stacked, manure hauled.

Some days I do just the one thing that needs doing most, whatever it happens to be that day. But many mornings I leave the house and find myself, hours later, in a trance of physical labor, covered in sawdust or mud or sweat, muttering quietly to myself. This is the very work I hated as a kid, the thing I dreaded whenever my dad came into a room where I sat reading. "I need some help," he would say and then walk out the door ahead of me, a little slumped in the shoulder, perhaps from knowing how grudging my help would be. It's not grudging now. I used to believe you could choose your influences. That's the principle behind every rebellion. Now I know that they choose you.

A few years ago I learned that my dad had consulted seriously with his father before moving to California in 1966. It was a small detail, but it reminded me that his life was not just an adjunct of my own. When I was young, he had always been in the public eye, even if it was only a small-town public. He was a bandleader—the man who stood at the conductor's podium in the high school gym, who directed summer concerts in the town park band shell, whose white, gold-braided band uniform hung stiffly in the closet. I had watched him playing cards with his wry farming brothers, their wit more caustic than his own, with a gift for irony that he has never had. I had seen his perennial optimism—his self-assurance. I noticed how readily people turned to him for practical advice and how sound that advice usually was. He tended to exaggerate, and he had a hard time admitting the limits of what he knew, but whenever I noticed those things he was in the presence of his smart-ass kid. From time to time, when I was still a boy, he took me outside town to visit farmers he knew—men whose children he had taught to play clarinet or drums. Those farms awoke a different man in him, the same one I saw working in the woodshop or garden. I was so bent on avoiding that work when I was young that I never wondered how my dad had learned to do it or what part it might have played in an inner life that was truly his own.

Until he left home for college in 1943, my dad followed his dad into the predawn darkness in work clothes every morning, headed for the dairy barn or the machine shed, a map of the day and its connection to other days already in my grandfather's mind. I barely remember seeing my grandfather at work on the farm, only an image of watching him turn in the seat of an old Farmall tractor while shelling corn in the late autumn or winter. The farm, when I first knew it, was still very much what he had made it over the years, though he lived in town by then. But when he and I drove out to the farm from town, I felt acutely that I was coming as a visitor and that my grandfather was arriving himself in visitor's clothing. His familiarity with the families, most of them relatives, who lived behind the windbreaks on the horizon, his keen appraisal of the crops in the fields and the condition of the cattle and hogs, the intimacy with which he knew the farmland itself—that was simply lost on me.

But "intimacy" is probably not a word my grandfather would have used to describe the way he knew his land. Intimacy implies too equal a balance between farmer and farm and not enough subjection of the soil. It's also too private a word. There's something public about the open terrain of northwest Iowa, something public too about the progressive way my grandfather farmed, as well as the role he took in George, a town his own father, who emigrated from Germany at eighteen in 1884, had helped found. What my grandfather really possessed was an intimate acquaintance with the character of his own labor, a private, unspoken awareness of how far he could push himself, how strong he was, where he was weak, and what work gave him greatest satisfaction. The intimacy with which he knew his land was really a reflection of the intimacy with which he knew himself. Both kinds of knowledge were tempered by self-expectation rooted in a roundly public sense of community whose social topography was defined by close kinship, the presence of so much family, so many Klinkenborgs. All these things were fostered, in one way or another, in his children.

When I returned to California in 1978 to help my parents raise the frame of their new house, I saw that for the first time in my life, and perhaps in his life too, my dad had found a scale of living—a landscape for his labor—that matched the scale of self-expectation he had seen in his father. Dad no longer owned just a house and yard, but a place we began, half-joking, to call the ranch. Working at the building site that summer, every one of us knew that some inner tension in the family had been released, a prospect enlarged, a dead end narrowly averted. In 1966, when we arrived from Iowa, Sacramento was a rough, unreconnoitered city only apparently gentled by the presence of so many government offices. By the time my parents moved to the edge of the mountains a dozen years later, a paralytic blandness had settled over the city and its cul-de-sac suburbs, a blandness as palling as the tule fogs that blind the San Joaquin Valley every winter. But on thirteen acres high above the fog, under a canopy of ponderosa pines along the Georgetown Divide, my father rebuilt a warm-weather version of his childhood, complete with cattle, sheep, hogs, chickens, tractors, and the obligation to walk out onto the land in his work clothes—a short-sleeved shirt and a pair of grease- or pitch-stained pants—every day when he was done with school. And by rebuilding his childhood he reframed the rest of my adulthood.

If I counted all the days I spent working beside my father at the ranch over the past twenty-five years, they would total only three or four months. And if I tried to make a list of the things he taught me direct-ly in that time, it would be a short one. There wasn't much to teach in most of the work we did together in those years. Burning a brush pile doesn't have many fine points. And, as we both learned long ago, my father and I are ill suited as teacher and student. He's impatient to move on to the next job, because he has a long list of jobs to finish before lunch, and I'm impatient because I know that some expert has written a book or an article about whatever we're doing which I can read at leisure. But every time I came home, something new had sprung up— an automated irrigation system, an apartment above the barn, a carport, a gazebo, new roof, new paint. The number of animals rose and fell and rose again. And soon, enough time had passed for decay to set in, for the first fences we built there to look run-down, like relics of a forgot-ten California. All the things Dad intended to do on the ranch began to coexist in an almost melancholy way with all the things he actually did.

When you take on a property like the one my parents bought—thir-teen rolling acres divided by a narrow irrigation ditch, broken by veins of rock, and covered in poison oak and head-high Scotch broom—you simply set out to clear the land and find a building site. But you leave traces of yourself with every decision you make, every fence you build, every tree you fell or plant, every quarter-acre you choose to irrigate or leave dry. In twenty years' time, a self-portrait emerges, and it exposes all the subtleties of your character, whether you like it or not. The land and the shape of the buildings show precisely how much disorder you can tolerate, how many corners you tend to cut, how much you think you can hide from yourself. Neatness may reflect nothing more than a passion for neatness, or it may be a sign of small ambitions. And beyond the literal landscape—the one that has been tilled and planted or logged or fenced or simply let alone—there is the ideal landscape that lives only in the mind. Every day you explore the difference between the two, knowing that you can see what no one else can.

At the ranch I could walk in a minute or two from the lightest, most orderly region of my father's personality—the woodshop or the apple orchard—across the irrigation ditch and down to a subliminal clutter of welding rods and oilcans and greasy tractor parts in the dark precincts of the barn. In a corner near the highway lay a part of the property my dad almost never visited, a dry, dusty tangle of raspberry brambles that must have pained him whenever he passed it on his way to the mailbox. Just a hundred yards off lay a grassy, well-watered ridge where he must have looked up from his work sometimes and marveled, as I did, at what he had made of this property. If you drove in the upper driveway, you came to a rose garden and a well-kept lawn. If you took the lower driveway, you found fuel tanks standing by a dilapidated corral, grass growing through the frame of an old sawmill, a sun-blistered camper shell resting on blocks. But I never once came to visit without seeing in those things the profusion and self-confidence of my father's character. I hope the mess I make speaks well of me someday.

DAD IS NOW SEVENTY-SIX, healthy, vigorous, almost adolescent, as seventy-six-year-olds tend to be these days. A couple of years ago, just before my stepmother's health failed, my parents sold the ranch and moved back down the mountain to a new development on the outskirts of Sacramento. They bought a house not one stick of which they put up themselves, and my dad started saying what a relief it was to have so little yard work to do. Now that I have a small farm of my own, I almost believe him. Still, my dad added a screen porch to the new house himself. He planted tomatoes where his neighbors might have hired a gardener to plant camellias.

It had never occurred to me that the ranch would be sold while my parents were alive. I felt the way I did when I learned that my grandmother's house in Iowa was being put up for sale, the way I'll feel if the home farm near George ever leaves the family. Every day I miss the ranch, not for its beauty alone, but because it was so inexpressibly of the people who made it. It was home to a part of me I didn't know existed until the summer we built the house there. That June, my brother John and I camped out on the foundation, lying awake late at night to watch the stars overhead. My arms were tight from hammering all day long, my back brown. The thought that in a few weeks I would return to the East Coast and a life among books and letters—a life purely of my own choosing—was inadmissible. Some of Dad's friends came to work on the house with us, and I was surprised to discover that my impatience with their ineptitude was more than matched by my father's impatience with them too. It was the first sign in years of how much we had in common, or rather it was the first sign I was willing to accept.

This farm of mine—these few bony acres—is the estate I've inherited from my father, a landscape both tangible and intangible. That's how I think of it. It's a way of propagating what I've learned about him and myself. It carries me back to a time when I was very young, standing at the edge of the garden in a small Iowa town watching him work a hive of bees. He wore white coveralls, a helmet and veil, and he stood on a stepladder because the hive was so tall, the honey flow from the surrounding farm fields so heavy. When Dad was here last June, one of the first things we did was walk down to look at the beehives on the edge of the garden. Then we worked together for a couple of days building a run-in shed for the horses. But as we set posts and measured rafters, I realized that I wanted to be building *his* run-in shed, not mine. I wanted to be adding another structure to a property he no longer owned, assuring a continuity of man and landscape that would last another thirty or forty years. I knew then that I would have to go on with this work alone, that someday it would have to be both father and son to me.

"I was one step removed from the farm," says writer Verlyn Klinkenborg. "My dad was a farm kid, my mom was a farm kid, all my aunts and uncles were farmers, but I grew up in a small town in Iowa, and any farmer knows that a town kid is not a farm kid in a serious way." Born in Colorado in 1952, Klinkenborg spent summers as a little boy on his uncles' farms. "That's where I learned the little bit that I know about how they actually lived and how they actually worked."

When Klinkenborg was 14, his family moved from Iowa to California, where he later graduated from Pomona College. After spending a year in Europe, he headed to Princeton for a Ph.D. in English literature. In 1978 he went to work as a curatorial assistant in literary and historical manuscripts at New York City's Pierpont-Morgan library.

The Rural Life *(2003) is a collection of essays that first appeared in* The New York Times, *on whose editorial board Klinkenborg has served since 1997. The essays chronicle his observations of country life as the seasons change, not only on his own five-acre farm in upstate New York (where he lives with his wife ad their dogs, cats, horses, and chickens) but also in Colorado, Wyoming, and various points west.*

"As a boy in Iowa," he says, "I would've never thought of going east. The only direction to go was west. It just never even occurred to me. So it's odd that I'm here."

Describing himself as "the private watcher of a small patch of ground," Klinkenborg finds the close study of nature an antidote to the hectic demands of the modern world. "My plan in buying this small farm wasn't to tutor the pasture and the sugar maples and the hemlocks," Klinkenborg writes. "I hoped instead to let the landscape tutor me."

Tina McElroy Ansa

You Know Better

S o that's just what I did. I put the vehicle into drive and pulled away from the curb with Miss Moses, her two sweaters, her four bags, her croaker sack, her umbrella, and her hat with the large cabbage rose on top safely at my side.

I know most folks would have thought, Lily Paine Pines, have you lost your mind? You find a confused old blind woman wandering around by herself in downtown Mulberry in the middle of the night, and you just pick her up and continue to drive around looking up and down alleys for your granddaughter?

And I'd have to say, "Well, yeah!"

And if someone had asked me why, I could not have told them. It's not as if LaShawndra were a child. She was almost nineteen years old.

Nineteen. Humph. When I was nineteen, I was handling a baby, a full freshman course load at Mulberry College, a part-time job, and a leadership position in the civil rights movement in Mulberry. But I try not to judge LaShawndra by my standards. She's a little individual, and she's had her own accomplishments.

She no longer lived at home.

She had a job—even if it was one as a part-time receptionist that I had gotten for her at the offices of the county school board where I'm the administrator.

She had her own place. Actually, she had moved into her friend Crystal's place. But she paid rent and was responsible for her share of other expenses. Oh, I helped her out a bit from time to time, but she was her own little woman.

But she was still my only granddaughter. It was after 1:00 A.M. I had no idea where she was. But I cannot tell you how much better I felt sitting up in that car with that old lady riding shotgun next to me.

We didn't talk for a while. To be honest, conversation just did not seem necessary. My ex-husband, Charles, and I were like that a bit. We could sit for hours and hold a conversation in our very own way without saying a word.

He would look at me, and I'd look at him. Then we'd fall out laughing. Or I'd just shrug my shoulders over something I'd read in the newspaper, and he'd nod his head in understanding. Or he'd wake me up in the middle of a late spring night and I would know what it was for even before he'd say, "Wake up, Lily. Smell the jasmine," as the sweet white scent wafted over us in bed from the vines growing on the trellis outside the window.

I do miss that camaraderie.

Charles and I have been divorced six years now, this second time. He's been out of my house for almost seven. But I still miss his presence and his ways.

My maiden name is Paine, and Charles's name is Pines. I always say, "I was born a Paine, but I'm going to die a Pines." And it looks like that's going to be the truth, because even though I do have a number of men friends, none of them is able to hold a candle to Charles, even if we couldn't seem to make it together.

But then black men as a whole are having such a difficult time holding it all together. My daughter, Sandra, doesn't think I understand about black men—bless her heart, like she does!—but I know the ponderous burden they carry around. Such *baggage!* Their pasts, their insecurities, their penises!

Charles wasn't an educated man. But he was a craftsman, a fine one, too. A master carpenter.

The first time I saw him striding along the rafters of the skeleton of a house two stories above the street, his leather tool belt slung low on his narrow hips—they were narrow then—his dazzling white short-sleeved T-shirt tucked tightly into the waistband of his jeans, I almost lost *my* balance with my two feet planted firmly on the ground. It was the sexiest image I had ever seen. He was so manly, so in charge.

Of course, we had known each other since childhood, but I had never been to one of his father's building sites where he helped out some Saturday afternoons. Since I was a preteen, Saturday has always been my "volunteer/give back to the community" day. So I was busy myself.

I had never in my life seen a man so sure of his step. So self-confident. And at the time Charles was really just a boy still in high school. I bet I stood there on Pringle Street in East Mulberry looking at him for an hour. Even from down on the street I could hear the little tune he always hummed to himself as he hammered and measured and stroked the wood. I can still remember what he smelled like—sweat and Lifebuoy soap—when he came down to greet me, put his strong, sweaty young arm around me, and show me off to the other workers.

But even those times that Charles smelled like sweat and dirt and a hard day's work when he came home from the construction site, he still smelled good to me. It's funny how we put up with funky smells from someone we love and sleep with that we wouldn't abide from a stranger. Even grow to like the funk. Heh, funny.

Of course, I do have some male friends now who I see from time to time. We Pines women just seem to attract men. Well, some of us do. But my current relationships, even the intimate ones, are nothing like what I had with Charles.

As LaShawndra says: Annnnnyway…

I chose to drive on out Broadway, since that was the way the car seemed to be headed.

At the corner of Broadway and Jackson, I thought of Charles again. No matter how I tried, Charles played in my mind all the time. Even now with us apart seven years.

Sandra wouldn't admit it, but she is a big daddy's girl. Charles thought the world of her from the moment she entered the world. He once told me that he knew, *knew,* the only reason I decided to settle down and marry him was because of Sandra.

And, you know, he was right. Toward the end of our second marriage we just clung to each other for the familiarity. He knew what I was thinking. What I needed. What I wanted. He knew me so well. Still does. Now he just gives me room.

At first it was a scary thought. I could not remember a time in which Charles Pines did not love me. He always seemed to know we would be together. Even after we got our first divorce, he just calmly went about his life in the interim, waiting to get back together with me. It was almost eerie watching him wait for me to come back around.

When he'd call to talk to Sandra or even when he would drive down from Atlanta to visit with her, he wouldn't even ask about what I had been doing lately for fear I'd take it the wrong way.

He never wavered from his certainty. I think he's doing the same thing now. But I do believe he is wrong. I won't be back again this time around. I will not. I will not. I will not.

As WE PAUSED at the stop sign on Jackson Street, I looked in the dimly lit dusty window of the army-navy surplus store on the corner. Charles brought Sandra there to buy her an authentic pea jacket to take away to college before we found out she was pregnant with LaShawndra.

Sandra and her daddy used to do a great many things together. In the fall she and Charles would go to the fair together, and both of them would come back all sticky with cotton candy and candied apples and a little sick to their stomachs from too many foot-long hotdogs. You know that daddy-daughter thing. It's so big you have to get out the way sometimes. And Charles always was a good daddy. I was proud of him for that. I'm sure I told him.

When Miss Moses and I passed the old train terminal with newly planted peach trees lining a garden at the entranceway, I could almost still hear the engines roaring in and out of Mulberry on the Macon-Dublin-Savannah line. Now you have to go over to Macon to catch the train going north or south. Back in the early eighties the city of Mulberry restored the old Gothic-style station and put little shops there, but it didn't take off, because the place doesn't even smell like trains anymore.

"I remember when they built that place," Miss Moses said, almost to herself. "I bet they still got up that big granite sign engraved with the word 'colored' over the side door."

I had a thousand questions about that time—I'm a bit of a historian myself. My mother was, too. She had biographies and history books all over the house. But Miss Moses didn't seem much for conversation. And she appeared to be comfortable and all buckled in to the passenger's side. So I didn't ask the questions that immediately bubbled up. I figured, why disturb her comfort with a legion of questions the answers to which she probably could not remember anyway.

I just looked over at Miss Moses and smiled.

She smiled back at me, then turned her sunglasses back to the road ahead as if she could see. I pressed on out Broadway, thinking, That was strange. I was not able to pinpoint exactly what had seemed off. The whole morning seemed off.

A little more than an hour before, I had been lying in my bed sleeping soundly—I always slept soundly—when, at the stroke of midnight, my eyes just flew open like shutters. You know how you wake up suddenly, as if someone had whispered your name and shaken you awake. That's exactly what had happened. Except the voice did not whisper. It bellowed.

And I could have sworn I had felt an icy hand press down on my left shoulder. The thing was, I was alone in my house on Oglethorpe Street. I was still a bit groggy, but when I looked down, I did see a hand on my shoulder. It was brown and old and wrinkled, the nails clipped to a medium length, thick and grayish. I've felt and sensed things all my life. My mother used to call me "my little sensitive child" because I just seemed to feel things deeply. But you know how mothers are about their children. My mother thought I was as cute and smart as they came. It helps to have someone think that about you.

As a child, I'd say, "Grandmama's coming today." And sure enough my mother's mother would arrive for a surprise visit from the country. Or I'd warn, "Mama, be real careful while you cooking," and before the sun set that day, my mother would have burned her hand on a big hot black cast-iron skillet.

Sometimes Mama would even bring me to Grandmama's bed and ask me to lay my hands on her arthritic knees and ankles. After a while

Grandmama would sigh and smile and say, "Thank you, baby. Grandmama's knees feel a lot better." But I always thought she was just saying that to humor her favorite grandchild. Or that the healing was all in Grandmama's head.

The hand on my shoulder, however, was no illusion. It might have looked old, but there was strength in that hand. It shook me awake, and a voice that sounded like Yahweh speaking to Moses in the desert said, "Get up and go forth!"

Needless to say, I woke up.

At first I tried to pretend that perhaps it had been my cat, Honey, walking across my chest, mewing in my ear, wanting me to get up and give her a dried-shrimp treat, but when I looked down toward the foot of my bed, my old honey-colored cat was curled up there sound asleep.

I yearned to ignore that cold hand and that wake-up call.

It was barely midnight, but I knew I did not want to face that day. Because I could feel deep in my soul, in that space between your breasts and your navel—that spot, your gut, your intuitive self, your knowing place—right there I could feel that this day that had not even yet dawned was going to be one that tried my very faith.

But I did not tarry there for even a moment in my nice soft, warm, freshly changed bed—I had just received a lovely rose-colored down comforter by FedEx that I had ordered for myself, and it was a chilly hour. I did not even consider if what I was feeling was real or just the residue of some upsetting dream that I could neither remember fully nor completely forget. I try to honor my commitments and my intuitions. Besides, I knew that the cold hand on my shoulder was no dream. Even completely awake, I continued to feel the chill from that wrinkled otherworldly hand spread down my left arm like a heart attack. I knew, if nothing else, that it was time for me to, as my mama always said, put my knees to the floor. I just rolled out of bed and landed in a supplicant's position.

Kneeling there beside my bed, at my low altar, I lit a stick of frankincense. The Word still on my lips, I fervently prayed that the fragrance would lift souls up to heaven. My first mind told me I would truly need heavenly help to conquer this day.

I've learned not to doubt my first mind. You can't go wrong following your first mind. I had discovered that over the years.

My first mind was never wrong. I believe that has contributed to the sheer number of projects and accomplishments over my life—teaching, raising a family, volunteering in the community, traveling to my favorite village on the coast of Sardinia, chairing charity committees here in Mulberry, sponsoring a student at my alma mater each semester, putting in a full vegetable garden each spring and fall in my backyard. And fifty-seven isn't all that old in the world we live in now. Except for gravity lowering my butt and titties, I do very well, thank you. And I make up my mind, and I stick to my decision.

That morning as I knelt on the long narrow foam pad I had covered myself with burgundy leather, knelt there in silence at my little altar covered with a clean white cloth, my first mind spoke to me, spoke to me clearly. It said LaShawndra, my granddaughter, my only grandbaby, was about to fall into deep trouble.

I closed my eyes and prayed like Hannah or someone else from the Old Testament. I felt myself swaying and rocking on my knees. Then a little irritation like a tickle started in the back of my throat, and before I knew anything, a small guttural sound replaced the tickle there. Then, again before I knew it, a humming was emanating from beneath my throat, from somewhere near the depths of my soul.

My mouth automatically began moving. "Jesus, Jesus, Jesus," I chanted over and over. I was seeking succor and an answer to my pleas. "Help my little granddaughter. I got such a bad feeling she's in trouble. She may just be a little hoochie mama, but she's my child, Lord. And she's yours, too. You know and understand hot women like her. So save her!"

I only have the one grandchild. A girl. I only had one little ole big-eyed girl. That's Sandra. And she only had one little ole big-eyed girl. That's LaShawndra. But even so, I've always felt blessed. Many of my friends' grandchildren may have done better scholastically and professionally than my LaShawndra, but they don't have the drive and the fire that mine has. Of course, LaShawndra could stand to learn some discipline, and it wouldn't hurt her to use some of the social graces I've taught her, but you can't beat her spirit.

Even though it was after midnight, I reached for the nearest portable phone and hit number one on the speed dial. I knew that Crystal and her two children would be in bed at that hour. Crystal's a good mother.

She answered the phone on the first ring. I could hear the sleep in her voice, but she perked up when she recognized mine.

"Mrs. Pines?" she said. "What is it? Is everything okay?"

I knew that LaShawndra probably wouldn't be there at home. She stays in the street so much. But I had to find out. Crystal knew that my granddaughter was out when she answered the phone, I could tell by her tone, but she still got out of bed and went to LaShawndra's bedroom next to hers and double-checked for me.

"I'm sorry, Mrs. Pines, LaShawndra isn't in," Crystal said after a bit, trying to make her voice sound neutral. "I think she was planning to go to The Club tonight. And she may be spending the night with a girl-friend. Do you want to leave a message for her?"

I knew good and well LaShawndra was not hardly staying overnight with a "girlfriend." But all I said was "Just tell her to give me a call when you see her. Okay, dear?" I saw no reason to upset Crystal for no more reason than my unsettling midnight feelings.

Looking back on that morning, I wish now I had been psychic and told Crystal to grab her babies and get out of that apartment as fast as she could. But like I say, I'm not clairvoyant, so I didn't give a word of warning.

Crystal is a good girl to be a mother of two barely out of her teens. So is LaShawndra… a good girl… in her own way. It's her spirit that gets her in trouble so much.

It was LaShawndra's fiery spirit that I saw and felt in every nook and cranny of my house on Oglethorpe Street as I got ready to go look for her. She had been with me so much of her life—up until about a year ago, when she moved out—staying overnight or over the weekend or all week, or even for months sometimes, that there seemed to be imprints of her stamped all over my house.

As I quickly combed and brushed my long nappy hair, black with just a few flecks of gray, into a chignon—my colleagues call it my "signature chignon"—at the dressing table in my bedroom, I saw LaShawndra at age four, sitting there on that same sturdy wooden stool, her little bare feet, toenails painted pink, poking through the old lace cover, trying to imitate me.

Of course, her mother, Sandra, had given the child a perm already, at the age of four, to, as Sandra put it, "smooth out some of LaShawndra's rough edges." So even as a toddler LaShawndra wouldn't just play with the brush—getting her hair all caught up and twisted in the bristles. She would *style* her hair. Like a grown woman. She has a knack for that. Anything to do with enhancing one's looks. She even started combing my hair when she was only about six or seven. She always wanted me to wear it loose and wild. So she'd comb it into all kinds of styles—multiple Afro puffs, a nappy pageboy, hundreds of tiny braids with the ends loose and bushy. All kinds of styles. But when she finished, she'd always brush it back from my face—no bangs, no baby hair coaxed down from the edges—and then twist it back into this bun at the nape of my neck. Same way I wear it now.

Bless her little vocational-school heart, LaShawndra has always had a way with hair. She thought it was funny that I didn't straighten my hair and instead wore it long and natural.

My hair has never had a chemical in it in its life. Nothing to straighten out the nap. I was the first girl in Mulberry to wear a natural. We called it a "bush" back then in the sixties. Virgin black hair. Shoot, my hair is like a person all on her own. I read a magazine article in which Sonia Braga—you know, the Brazilian actress with all that great wild hair—she said, referring to her own hair, "She loves for me to wash her and let her dry in the sun." That's how I feel about my hair.

And that's what I do sometimes: I wash her, rinse her in rainwater that I catch in a wooden barrel at the southeastern corner of my house, and sit out on my patio off the kitchen to let her dry in the sun.

But when you're worrying about your own flesh and blood, those things—like your daily toilette—seem rather trivial. For the same reason, I didn't stop to stretch my body on my Pilates machine before I left the bedroom. I've been practicing yoga since I was a teenager, but in recent years, I've moved to Pilates training. I *love* my Pilates.

But even while I washed up, brushed my hair, and pulled on a bra, a big beige cotton sweater, and some black slacks, I continued to pray. By the time I took my soft black moccasins from the shoe rack in my closet, I was chanting to myself under my breath. But through my praying and my chanting, I was trying to get to my granddaughter before it was too late. Too late for what, I wasn't clear about just then, but that didn't decrease the urgency I felt one bit.

I didn't even take time to stop and stand in front of a full-length mirror to make sure I looked as good going as I did coming.

It was a small hint that my mama had taught me when I was about thirteen years old. So here it was, forty-four years later, and whenever I'm headed out the door, I'm still asking myself, Now, how does my butt look? Do I have any VPL—visible panty lines? Is my skirt so tight it's cupping under my butt? Is my slip hanging? Can you see my bra straps peeking over my shoulder?

I've been doing it for so long, I do it without even thinking. But I guess that morning my mind was more on my grandchild, LaShawndra. I didn't much care about visible panty lines. She would have understood that.

When I had passed on the little hint of a last mirror check to the child, she said, just as seriously, "But, Mama Mama, sometimes I *want* my bra straps or my panties to show."

Lord help us all!

Born the youngest of five children in Macon, Georgia, in 1949, Tina McElroy Ansa grew up listening to her grandfather tell ghost stories on the porch at home. She also paid close attention as strangers spun stories in her father's juke joint downtown. "In the South of the 1950s and 1960s, where I was raised," Ansa says, "Black folks talked all the time about spirits and hants, dreams and visions, feelings and ghost tales that were true."

In her fourth novel, You Know Better (2002), three generations of women receive some unsolicited help from the town's spirits as they try to solve their problems. "I hear people telling young people all the time: 'You know better,'" Ansa says. "But they don't know better. Our generation has dropped the ball with our young people. We haven't taught them better."

After graduating from Spelman College in 1971 with a degree in English, Ansa became the first African-American woman to work at the Atlanta Constitution; there, and later at the Charlotte Observer, she worked as a copy editor, reporter, features writer, and layout editor. In 1982 she began a full-time freelance career, publishing short stories, novels, articles, and essays.

"One of the things that I love to write about in fiction is family," she says. "The patterns, the leitmotifs in families… are the things that truly touch me about people." Ansa lives on St. Simons Island, Georgia, with her husband, the filmmaker Jonée Ansa.

Alma Luz Villanueva

Luna's California Poppies

MID-JUNE… CALIFORNIA POPPIES ALL OVER THE FIELDS!!!!
Dear La Virgen,

L ast night a neighbor across the road, and up from Sally—the houses are separated by FIELDS here—this guy woke me up. He was obviously plastered and yelling something at the top of his lungs. Sally had warned me, "He's the most arrested man in Sonoma County as he's a drunk and sometimes he beats his wife, a good woman too and a damned shame, her with six children to feed. Well, the county helps her out I'm told, someone's got to." For a second I wanted to tell her about my ex-husband, how I had to be on welfare for awhile to <u>survive</u> and go to school, but I decided not to considering how gossip can spread in a small town—exactly the way she's telling me about them, right?

So, I woke up to The Most Arrested Man in Sonoma County yelling something, and I mean he was YELLING at about 2 am. I picked my way through the dark, checking my kids as they slept through it. I opened the back door to hear him better, what the hell he was shouting about, and the soft summer air was so sweet and tangled with unnamable things somewhere out there in the dark, tears sprang to my eyes. I had actually been ready to scream, "SHUT UP!" But the night took me by surprise, it was so soft, and I sat down on the top step and just listened for awhile. And finally I heard it. He was quoting a poem, Dylan Thomas. (I studied his poetry in school and his book's in my book shelf in the front room.) I recognized the first stanza and just followed his voice, which was thick with hooch and a thick Irish brogue (he must be Irish). I was amazed and enthralled—The Most Arrested Man in Sonoma County seemed to know whole poems by heart, by memory, unless he was reading it, but I couldn't see any lights on his porch, where he obviously was standing in absolute darkness at 2 am yelling wonderful poetry. So I just listened, Virgen, sitting on the top step of my dark porch, breathing in the soft, sweet, unnameable things of summer. June. Almost my daughter's 13th birthday. I was tempted to wake her up to hear him, but then I knew she'd wonder if living on the farm for almost 3 months had made me go koo-koo (if she only knew, right Virgen?)—so I didn't.

And his voice kept breaking my heart, it was so full of defeated longing. At the end of each line it sounded like he was going to give it up, but then he'd come back with a ROAR. Here's the first stanza of my favorite one, and the last poem he shouted:

"I see the boys of summer in their ruin
Lay the gold tithings barren,
Setting no store by harvest, freeze the soils;
There in their heat the winter floods
Of frozen loves they fetch their girls,
And drown the cargoed apples in their tides."

It's a long poem, nine stanzas, and he'd been out there shouting poetry for at least 20 minutes, so when the cops arrived, no siren with just the slowly flashing lights, he was almost to the final stanza; he continued as they approached, and then he was just silent as they led him to the car.

I imagined his wife and kids were probably sadly relieved he was gone (he was so hooched), and I hope the only damage he'd committed that night was poetry. After the cop car floated away into the night toward jail, I went inside, found my flashlight and Dylan Thomas, and brought him out to the back porch. By flashlight I read the last stanza out loud—here it is:

> "I see you boys of summer in your ruin.
> Man in his maggot's barren.
> And boys are full and foreign in the pouch.
> I am the man your father was.
> We are the sons of flint and pitch.
> O see the poles are kissing as they cross."

Then I read the last stanza out loud, again and again, and each time it meant more to me, and tears just poured down my face. There's such grief in this poem, such sorrow, regret, and redemption. "O see the poles are kissing as they cross." Forgiveness. The cross. The fiery cross. Where it's thick and green now.

Virgen, you probably know it's been a long time since I've even talked to my mother Carmen, and it's been an even longer time that I've hated her. But sitting on the porch reading this stanza over and over, I remembered an old story Carmen told me when I was little, how she carried me as a baby of about 2 years, on a most likely unbearably hot summer day, down a dusty Louisiana road—she said it was summer and you could fry an egg by the sun—she carried me and her suitcase to a bus stop because neither my father nor his racist family—Carmen told me one time that she heard one of them say she was no better than a nigger—would drive her. And her choice was to leave me behind. But she didn't. She carried me all the way. To the bus stop. And home to Mamacita. So, I change the words to: "I am the woman your mother was. We are the daughters of flint and pitch. O see the poles are kissing as they cross." The cross. The fiery cross. Where it's green now.

And I think of the last time I saw her, when Whitey died (left his body)—how I couldn't stand her, and at the same time how I noticed her stubborn <u>spirit</u> was still entirely intact, and I realize clearly now at this moment that both things are true for me. I can't stand her, but I must know she's intact. (That I <u>must</u> love her… I am the woman your mother was.) That I'm <u>grateful</u> she carried me to the bus stop and brought me home to mi familia, Mamacita y Tía. (That she must've loved me… I am the woman your mother was.)

Finally, I read the whole poem through out loud from beginning to end—kind of wanting to yell it, but I'm not that brave, and that's the truth. My tears had stopped and it was as though I could see in the dark. Night Eyes like in Bolinas (remember?). And I knew I'd call Carmen. It will be very weird and awkward, but I know I have to do it, call her. (I haven't done it yet, but I will, I promise, Virgen.)

Then I carried the flashlight (but didn't use it) as I walked toward the creek and across the wooden bridge to the back fields where the hay is starting to get high. Sally advised me to put a steer or two back there for the meat, she said, and that they also eat the hay like automatic lawn mowers, plus they get nice and fat, she said, and healthy on all that good hay out back that's just growing for free. So maybe I will. But then of course we'd have to KILL the steers to eat them (whine whine)….

I bent down to see the California Poppies, but they were all closed up against the night and I imagined them dreaming about the SUN—how they open their fiery sunlike petals first thing in the morning. And then I suddenly heard the white lady teacher's voice, "It's against the LAW to pick California Poppies because they're the State Flower." How she glared her words into the eyes set into the brown and black faces—how she glared the words into my eyes. And I realized, 18 years later, what she really said—that it was against the law to love the sun, the moon and stars in the sky, the flowers and trees that grow on the earth for FREE, especially if you're poor and brown/black-skinned. It was against the law to trust your Secret Crystal World Dreams (if you had any)—to trust them (and never speak of them in that class, of course) but most of all, <u>most of all </u>it was against the law to love your OWN SELF. So, I picked a bunch of dreaming California Poppies and I ate one just like I did as a kid, La Loca.

There I was at probably going on 4 am in the morning in the middle of June, sitting in the back fields, and I wasn't afraid of the KKK, perverts, muggers or vampires for that matter. I ate another California Poppy and thought about the principal we just impeached at the junior high—I went to pick Tania up for the dentist, so while I waited for her I saw him drive off (his last day there) in his white Cadillac with a white interior, with his wife sitting next to him, and she had (no joke) <u>white hair</u> that looked so stiff it could've been cement the way the waves of her white hair obeyed her. I could only stare (and stare). And he was dressed ENTIRELY in white, though of course I couldn't see his shoes, but every time I saw him they were…I guess that was his final statement to us all, or maybe that's just the way he normally lived his life (free from all darkness and nigger-o lovers).

I ate another California Poppy and I thought about how we—the like-minded teachers and parents—also abolished "Slave Day" (believe it or not)—a practice of auctioning a student slave for a day to the highest bidder in the name of school funds and "good clean fun." They would actually stand a kid on a crate and auction him or her off—and the kid looked pretty embarrassed as the other ones really got into it in a nasty way, probably because it wasn't them being a slave, right? Tania came home and told me about it so I was there the next day with a group of other parents, then the teachers who heaved every year also spoke up. Anyway, I know this isn't ending racism here, but it feels like it might help, bit by BIT. Of course, I know the boys don't want anyone to know I'm their mother (The Trouble Maker), especially their new friends, but then I also know they count on me to do this stuff, secretly, like all's well in the world if Mom is being a pain in the ass to whoever currently needs it—but they actually duck down in the car not to be seen with me, and I pretend I don't notice for now.

I ate another California Poppy and remembered the very last time I talked to Whitey and he still understood me. I told him for the second and last time in my life that I loved him, right to his face, his mortified eyes. "Now don't go gettin mushy on me fer Christ's sake." But I could see how (secretly) pleased he was. And then I kissed him on the cheek, as he pretended to get away, but of course he was in the bed he'd die in (leave the body) within the week. My lips remember the feel of his cheek: fragile, temporary. Ripe wild rose petals.

I ate one more California Poppy and I heard myself speaking to Mamacita, welcoming her to this farm in Sebastopol, my home, my children's home, because I know she'd love it here. And then I started thinking about planting chilis, onions, scallions, tomatoes, squash, corn, and then I <u>knew</u> Mamacita was really here—and I swear to you, Virgen, I felt her SWELL up inside me and I thought of Dylan Thomas' words: "I am the woman your mother was." And then I felt Whitey swell up inside me too, so I welcomed him: "I am the man your father was." And I thought of his love of steaks and fried chicken with mashed potatoes, smothered in butter and gravy, on the side—so I decided to get 2 STEERS, some laying chickens and some FRYERS—those are male chickens you eat (kill). Sally said she'd help me figure all this out, the best places to buy them, even what you call these animals (pullets are fryers) when you actually grow them to be your food—whine, whine—I'm beginning to love this woman who picks out the layers who don't lay as much anymore for The Stew Pot, she says, because if you don't do it quick enough they get too tough to eat with any pleasure, and you just eat them not to waste food. So, for Sally: "We are the dark deniers, let us summon / Death from a summer woman." (The same poem.)

How can I ever thank The Most Arrested Man in Sonoma County for this night, Virgen? I just wish he didn't beat his wife and terrorize his children—a California Poppy for each of them. But I am grateful for his muy crazy (brave) self that woke me up and kept me up till DAWN reading Dylan Thomas' poems (poems I haven't read in years), and writing one of my OWN....

The author of the award-winning novels The Ultraviolet Sky *(1989 American Book Award, Before Columbus Foundation) and* Naked Ladies *(1994 PEN Oakland Josephine Miles Award), Alma Luz Villanueva was born in Lompoc, California, in 1944. She grew up in the Mission district of San Francisco, where she lived with her Yaqui grandmother, Jesus Villanueva, until she was 11 years old.*

"Jesus taught me to recite poetry by heart (in Spanish) for church and she often read me poetry in Spanish," Villanueva has said. "So, though I write in English, the language/meaning is rooted in Spanish." After her grandmother died, Alma Luz was raised by her mother, Lydia Villanueva, and aunt, Ruth Villanueva. She never knew her father, but later learned he was of German ancestry.

Although Villanueva's early poems drew from her poverty-stricken childhood, they also describe the love, perseverance, and strength of the female community around her. Reviewers have noted that Villanueva's work often uses the wisdom of her Yaqui culture to guide her female characters in a world dominated by males and the Anglo culture.

Luna's California Poppies *(2002) takes the form of a diary, addressed to the Virgin of Guadalupe, written by Luna Luz Villalobos as she grows from child to adult. Like Villanueva, Luna finds both solace and strength in her writing.*

Villanueva dropped out of school in 10th grade to have the first of her four children; her second was born when she was 17. Married to a violent man, she lived on welfare in a public housing project in San Francisco. "I didn't write anything from age 13 to 26," she once said, "because I was struggling for survival."

Eventually Villanueva completed a post-secondary education at City College of San Francisco and Norwich University. In 1984 she earned her M.F.A. from Vermont College. She has been writer-in-residence at University of California at Irvine, Stanford University, and the University of California at Santa Cruz. She currently lives in San Miguel de Allende, Mexico.

Robert Stone

Bay of Souls

For a while they talked about populism and guns and militia-men. They had fallen silent in the dimming light when Alvin put a delaying hand on Michael's arm. Everyone stopped where they stood. There were deer, four of them, an eight-point buck and three females. One of the females looked little older than a year-ling. The deer were drinking from the icy river, upstream, upwind. The three men began to ease closer to the stream, where a bend would provide them a clear line of fire. The deer were something more than thirty-five yards away. Michael tried shuffling through the snow, which was topped with a thin frozen layer, just thick enough ice to sound underfoot. He stepped on a frozen stick. It cracked. One of the does looked up and in their direction, then returned to her drinking. Finally, they came to a point beyond the tree line and looked at one another.

The target of choice would be the big buck. If they were after meat, the does, even the youngest, were legal game. The buck was splashing his way to the edge of deep water. In a moment all four of the deer tensed in place, ears up. A doe bent her foreleg, ready to spring. There was no more time. Everyone raised his weapon. Michael, without a scope, found himself sighting the shoulder of the buck. It was a beautiful animal. Magical in the fading light. Things change, he thought. Everything changes. His finger was on the trigger. When the other men fired, he did not. He had no clear idea why. Maybe the experience of having a man in his sights that day.

The buck raised his head and took a step forward. His forelegs buckled, and he shifted his hindquarters so that somehow his hind legs might take up the weight being surrendered by his weakening body. Michael watched the creature's dying. It was always hard to watch their legs give way. You could feel it in your own. The pain and vertigo.

"If he falls in that stream," Norman said, "he'll float halfway to Sioux City."

But the animal staggered briefly toward the bank and toppled sidewise into the shallows. The does vanished without a sound.

"Did you take a shot?" Norman asked Michael. Michael shook his head.

Examining the kill, they found two shotgun wounds close to the animal's heart.

"Guess we both got him," Norman said.

"He's yours," said Alvin Mahoney. "You shot first."

Norman laughed. "No, man. We'll have the butcher divide him. Three ways."

Michael helped drag the dead deer by its antlers out of the water.

"Anybody want to mount that rack?" Norman asked.

"I don't think my wife would live with it," Michael told him.

"I wouldn't care to myself," Norman said. "Anyway, it's not trophy size."

They were only a short distance from the canoe, but it was dark by the time they had hauled the deer aboard. Paddling upriver, they came to the place where Michael had dropped his flashlight overboard. The beam was still soldiering on, illuminating the bottom of the stream.

They secured the buck to the hood of the Jeep and set out for the state highway. This time they did not stop at the Hunter's Supper Club but drove all the way to Ehrlich's to get the deer tagged. When they had finished the forms for Fish and Game, they went into the restaurant and sat down to dinner. Mahoney was the designated driver and abstained from drink. He would, Michael thought, make up for it at home. He and Norman had Scotch, but it was not nearly as good as the Willoughby's. Then they ordered a pitcher of beer.

The menu featured wurst, schnitzel, potato pancakes, noodles and dumplings. There were deer heads and antlers with brass plaques on the dark wood walls and scrolled mottos in gothic script. A polka was on the jukebox and the place was filled with hunters. At Ehrlich's many of the hunters had family members along. There were women and children, even babies. Happy couples danced. The entire place rejoiced in an atmosphere of good-hearted revelry.

"Boy, is this place ever different from the Hunter's," Michael said. "It's not just the food."

"Know why?" Norman asked.

"Different people," said Michael.

"Different folks," Norman said. "This is Prevost County. They're Germans here. They're peace-loving. Orderly. You gotta love 'em."

"Do you?"

"Sure. Whereas the Hunter's is in the fucking swamp. Harrison County. Irish, Scotch-Irish, French Canadian. They're poor and surly. They're over at the Hunter's getting nasty drunk and selling one another wolf tickets. While here, *hier ist fröhlich.*"

He spread his arms and with a cold, false smile enacted a parody of gemütlichkeit.

"Maybe we belong over there," Alvin Mahoney said.

Michael and Norman looked at each other and laughed.

Norman raised his beer glass. "Here's looking at you, Alvin," he said.

Alvin laughed. He was nervous, drinkless. It might be safer driving, Michael thought, to let him have a belt.

Michael was aware of Norman watching him. "You didn't shoot today," Norman said.

Michael shrugged.

As they were waiting for the check, Norman said, "I have to ask you something. Over at St. Emmerich's, what are they teaching my friend Paulie about abortion? Me, I don't think there's much wrong with the world that doesn't come from there being too many people."

Michael poured out the last of the beer.

"I'm sorry," Norman said. "You're the only person I know to ask."

For the second time Michael was annoyed with Norman. Of course, sociology was the man's job. And he had never been subtle or discreet. He had been to Vietnam. He owned the big questions.

"They don't talk about it," Michael said. "Not at that level." He put a paper napkin to a tiny puddle of foam on the table before him. "They talked about hunting the other day." What he said was not exactly true. Paul was being taught that life began at conception. The rest, of course, would follow. But Michael was not in the mood to defend the theses of St. Emmerich's Christian instruction. Embarrassed, he flushed and hid behind his beer. He felt besieged. As though they were trying to take something away from him. Something he was not even sure he possessed.

Because I believe, he thought. They know I believe. If I believe. But faith is not what you believe, he thought. Faith was something else.

A blond waitress with a pretty, wholesome smile came over to them but she did not have the check.

"Is one of you guys Michael Ahearn?" she asked.

"Me," Michael said.

"Sir, you got a phone call. Want to take it in the kitchen?"

He followed her across the room, resounding with polkas, laughter, the rattle of plates and foaming schooners. In the kitchen three generations of women, the oldest in her late sixties, the youngest a little older than his son, worked purposefully. The warm room smelled of vinegary marinades. His wife was on the phone.

"Michael," she said. Her voice was distant and, he thought, chill. It made him think of the woods. Or of the light shining at the bottom of the freezing stream. "Paul is not accounted for. He was at the gym and then I thought he was going to Jimmy Collings's. But he's not there. And his school books are here. And Olaf is missing." She paused. "It's snowing here."

He remembered the deer at the edge of the stream. Its life ebbing, legs giving way.

"I suppose I called for moral support," she said. "I'm afraid."

"Hang in," he told her.

He walked back through the noisy room. Alvin and Norman were paying the check. Michael went into his wallet, took out two twenties and threw them on the table.

"That's too much," Norman said.

"Kristin is worried about Paul. He's out late."

It was snowing on Ehrlich's parking lot when they got to the Jeep. Alvin checked the lines securing the carcass of the deer. Michael took a back seat.

"You know," Alvin said, "kids are always getting up to some caper and you get all hot and bothered and it's nothing."

It was the last thing anyone said on the ride home.

The snow came harder as they drove, slowing them down. Michael watched it fall. He thought of the man with the deer in his wheelbarrow. By gad, sir, you present a distressing spectacle. If he could make it up somehow. His thoughts had all been mean and low. What he did not want in his mind's eye now was his son's face, the face on which he so doted. But it was there after all and the boy under snow. Hang in.

"Did I pass out?" he asked them.

"You were sleeping," Norman said.

How could he sleep? He had slept but forgotten nothing. His boy had been there the whole time. Prayer. No. You did not pray for things. Prayers, like Franklin's key on a kite, attracted the lightning, burned out your mind and soul.

When, hours later, they drove into town there were dead deer hanging from the trees on everyone's lawn. The lawns were wide in that prairie town. They supported many trees, and almost every bare tree on almost every lawn in front of almost every house had a dead deer or even two, slung over the low boughs. There were bucks and does and fawns. All fair game, legal. There were too many deer.

A police car was blocking Michael's driveway. Norman parked the Jeep on the street, across the lawn from his front door. Everyone got out, and when they did the young town policeman, whom Michael knew, whose name was Vandervliet, climbed out of his cruiser.

"Sir," Vandervliet said, "they're not here. They're at MacIvor."

MacIvor was the tri-county hospital on the north edge of town.

Norman put a hand on his shoulder. Michael climbed into Vandervliet's Plymouth cruiser.

"What?" Michael asked the young cop. "Is my son alive?"

"Yessir, but he's suffering from exposure."

And it did not sound so good because as they both knew, the cold, at a certain point, was irreversible, and all the heat, the fire, the cocoa, hot-water bottles, sleeping bags, down jackets, quilts, whiskey, medicine, nothing could make a child stop trembling and his temperature rise.

"Your wife is injured, Professor. I mean, she ain't injured bad but she fell down trying to carry the boy I guess and so she's admitted also over there at MacIvor."

"I see," Michael said.

"See, the boy was looking for the dog 'cause the dog was out in the snow."

On the way to the hospital, Michael said, "I think I'm going to shoot that dog."

"I would," said Vandervliet.

At MacIvor, they were waiting for him. There was a nurse whose husband ran the Seattle-inspired coffee shop in town and a young doctor from back east. They looked so agitated, he went numb with fear. The doctor introduced himself but Michael heard none of it.

"Paul's vital signs are low," the doctor said. "We're hoping he'll respond. Unfortunately, he's not conscious, and we're concerned. We don't know how long he was outside in the storm."

Michael managed to speak. "His body temperature…?"

"That's a cause of concern," the doctor said. "That will have to show improvement."

Michael did not look at him.

"We can treat this," the doctor said. "We see it here. There's hope."

"Thank you," Michael said. Above all, he did not want to see the boy. That fair vision and he kept repelling it. He was afraid to watch Paul die, though surely even in death he would be beautiful.

"We'd like you to talk to... to your wife," the doctor said. "We're sure she has a fracture and she won't go to x-ray." He hesitated for a moment and went off down the corridor.

At MacIvor the passageways had the form of an X. As the doctor walked off down one bar of the pattern, Michael saw what appeared to be his wife at the end of the other. She was in a wheelchair. The nurse followed him as he walked toward her.

"She won't go to x-ray," the nurse complained. "Her leg's been splinted and she's had pain medication and we have a bed ready for her but she won't rest. She won't let the medication do its thing."

Kristin, huge-eyed and white as chalk, wheeled herself in their direction. But when Michael came up, the nurse in tow, she looked through him. There was an open Bible on her lap.

The nurse went to take the handles of Kristin's wheelchair. Michael stepped in and took them himself. Do its thing? He had trouble turning the wheelchair around. The rear wheels refused to straighten out. Do their thing. He pushed his wife toward the wall. Her splinted right leg extended straight out and when its foot touched the wall, she uttered a soft cry. Tears ran down her face.

"There's a little trick to it," said the nurse. She made a sound that was not quite a laugh. "Let me."

Michael ignored her. The wheelchair resisted his trembling pressure. Oh goddamn shit.

"Take me in to him," Kristin said.

"Better not," the nurse said, to Michael's relief.

If he could see himself, futilely trying to ambulate his wife on wheels, Michael thought, it would be funny. But hospitals never had mirrors. There was a discovery. In the place of undoings, where things came apart, your children changed to cadavers, you spun your wife in wheelies, no mirrors. The joke was on you but you did not have to watch yourself.

When they were in the room she said, "I fell carrying him. He was by the garden fence—I fell in the snow." He could picture her carrying

Paul up from the garden, tripping, slipping, stumbling. He took her icy hand but she withdrew it. "He was so cold."

"Lie down," he said. "Can you?"

"No, it hurts."

He stood and rang for the nurse.

Kristin took up the Bible as though she were entranced and began to read aloud.

"'Be merciful unto me, O God, be merciful unto me: for my soul trusteth in thee: yea, in the shadow of thy wings will I make my refuge.'"

Closing his eyes, he tried to hold on to the words. Listening to her read in her mother's strange featureless tone, he could imagine Luther's Bible the way her mother out on the plains must have heard it from her own parents. A psalm for fools in the snow. Really expecting nothing but cold and death in the shadow of those wings. Odin's raven.

"'Until these calamities be overpast, I will cry unto God most high.'"

Michael sat listening, despising the leaden resignation of his wife's prayer, its acceptance, surrender.

"'My soul is among lions,'" she read, "'and I lie even among them that are set on fire.'"

His impulse was flight. He sat there burning until the nurse came in. For some reason, she looked merry, confidential.

"I think we turned a corner," she said. "Michael! Kristin! I think we turned a corner."

Then the doctor entered quietly and they got Kristin into bed and she went under the medication. Even unconscious, her eyes were half open.

The doctor said you responded or you didn't, and Paul had responded. His temperature was going up. He was coming up. He would even get his fingers and toes back and his ethical little Christian brain going, it appeared. The doctor looked so relieved.

"You can have a minute while we get the gurney. We've gotta get her x-rayed pronto because she's got a broken leg there."

"You can see Paul," the nurse said. "He's sleeping. Real sleep now."

The doctor laughed. "It's very exhausting to half freeze to death."
"It would be," Michael said.

While they got the gurney, he looked into Kristin's half-open, tortured, long-lashed blue eyes and brushed the slightly graying black hair from them. With her long face and buck teeth she looked like the Christus on a Viking crucifix. Given her, he thought, given me, why didn't he die? Maybe he still will, Michael thought. The notion terrified him. He had stood up to make his escape when the orderlies came in to take Kristin away. Michael rubbed her cold hand.

The chapel was down at the end of the corridor. It had a kind of altar, stained-glass windows that opened on nothing, that were inlaid with clouds and doves and other fine inspirational things.

Michael had been afraid, for a while, that there was something out there, at the beginning and end of consciousness. An alpha and an omega to things. He had believed it for years on and off. And that night, he had felt certain, the fire would be visited on him. His boy would be taken away and he would know, know absolutely, the power of the most high. Its horrible providence. Its mysteries, its hide-and-seek, and lessons, and redefined top-secret mercies to be understood through prayer and meditation. But only at really special moments of rhapsody and ecstasy and O, wondrous clarity. Behold now behemoth. Who can draw Leviathan? Et cetera.

But now his son's life was saved. And the great thing had come of nothing, of absolutely nothing, out of a kaleidoscope, out of a Cracker Jack box. Every day its own flower, to every day its own stink and savor. Good old random singularity and you could exercise a proper revulsion for life's rank overabundance and everybody could have their rights and be happy.

And he could be a serious person, a grownup at last, and not worry over things that educated people had not troubled themselves with practically for centuries. Free at last and it didn't mean a thing and it would all be over, some things sooner than later. His marriage, for one, sealed in faith like the Sepulchral stone. Vain now. No one watched over us. Or rather we watched over each other. That was providence, what a relief. He turned his back on the inspirations of the chapel and went out to watch his lovely son survive another day.

◎ *A dark vision pervades many of Robert Stone's novels. But that darkness always serves a moral purpose, as Stone's characters wrestle with some of life's "big questions" and try to make judgments about how to live in the world. "Often those judgments are difficult and laced with incredible ambiguity," Stone has said, "but ambiguity is not the absence of morality. It's just a confusion about morality."*

Stone himself faced considerable confusions in his early years. He was born in Brooklyn in 1937 and raised by his mother, who worked as a chambermaid. His father had deserted the family, and the pressures proved too great for his mother, who was diagnosed with schizophrenia. She was institutionalized for several years, during which time Stone lived in a Catholic orphanage. They were reunited when Stone was nine and lived together in a series of boarding houses and welfare hotels until Stone dropped out of high school and joined the Navy.

He became a journalist during his time in the Navy and afterward attended New York University and worked as a copy boy at the New York Daily News. *His marriage to Janice Burr in 1959 prompted a brief move to New Orleans. Later, during the 1960s, Stone formed friendships with several Beat Generation personalities, including Ken Kesey. Stone himself was not immune to the drugs and alcohol that fueled much of the 1960s' social ferment.*

His debut novel, A Hall of Mirrors, *won a William Faulkner Foundation award for best first novel in 1967 and earned Stone a Guggenheim Fellowship that fully launched his career as a writer. His second novel,* Dog Soldiers, *won the 1975 National Book Award.*

Stone and his wife now divide their time between New York City and Key West. Stone credits writing with helping him weather the hard times. "Without writing I would have dried up and blown away. That was my discipline, what I lived for, finally. I never had a lot of ego. It got crushed when I was small. Writing was the one thing I had that was beautiful, the only thing that justified me, the only way in which I could provide something beyond my own gratification."

Wole Soyinka

Lost Poems

I think sometimes of poems I have lost –
Maybe their loss it was that saved the world – still
They do get lost, and I recall them only
When a fragment levitates behind
Discarded invoices, the black-rimmed notice
Of a last goodbye, a birth, a wedding invitation
And other milestones of a lesser kind.

The moment torments – why? Beyond
An instant's passion, dubious flash –
Satori in a bar, taxi or restaurant, an airport
Waiting lounge – that births the scribble
On a stained napkin, what cast of the ephemeral
Once resonates, then spurns the mind
The morning after? All that survives

Mimics a wrinkled petal pressed
Between pages of long-discarded books.
A falling leaf trapped briefly by the passing sun

It flashes, a mere shard of memory
But filled with wistful accusations
Of abandonment. Too late,

No life to it. The book is closed
The moment's exultation or despair
Drowned in wine rivers, shrivelled
In suns of greater wars. I turn
These scrapbooks of a moment's truth
To cinders, their curlings curse in smoke –
Once more fugitive beyond recall
Of usurper's summons by
The morning after.

I think of voices I have lost, and touches.
The fleeting brush of eyes that burrows
Deep within the heart of need, the pledge
Unspoken, the more than acts of faith
That forge an instant world in silent pact
With strangers – deeper, deeper bonds
Than the dearest love's embrace.

Written during a period of exile from his native Nigeria, Wole Soyinka's Samarkand: And Other Markets I Have Known *documents his thoughts on the world at the close of the 20th century. Using the metaphor of the ancient Silk Road marketplace of Samarkand, the Nobel prize-winning writer, playwright, and poet reflects on such themes as the past and present, travel, exile, the deaths of François Mitterand and Nigerian dissident Ken Saro-Wiwa, writers, and his own creative process. He has been called "one of the liveliest, most exciting writers in the world today," by* The New York Times.

Born in Western Nigeria and Yoruban by heritage, Soyinka won numerous scholarships in his native Nigeria before attending the University of Leeds in England, where he established his reputation as a playwright with The Swamp Dwellers *and* The Lion and the Jewel, *and formed the theater group "The 1960 Masks." In his first novel,* The Interpreters (1965), *six scholars debate the fate of Nigeria. A passionate chronicler of Nigeria's tumultuous political history, Soyinka was arrested in 1967 for writing an article that demanded a cease-fire in the Nigerian civil war. He was imprisoned for nearly two years, during which time he kept journals on scraps of toilet paper, written with ink he made himself. His memoir of the experience,* The Man Died: Prison Notes of Wole Soyinka, *won international acclaim.*

A champion of literature as an agent for social change, Soyinka in 1986 became the first African to win the Nobel Prize. He is the author of several volumes of essays—among them Myth, Literature, and the African World (1975)—*a handful of poetry collections, and the 2006 memoir* You Must Set Forth at Dawn.

5 | Wising Up

"To know how to grow old is the master-work of wisdom, and one of the most difficult chapters in the great art of living."

—Henri Frédéric Amiel

Maxine Hong Kingston

I Call on the Muses of Poetry, and Here's What I Get

March 22, the Third Day of Spring 2000
  Early morning, a bird is saying
    Me Me Me
    Do do do do

Birds

I'm living in one place so long,
the birds enlace their nests
with my white hair.

I'd like their recognizing me in return.
I play a game with hummingbirds.
I play the hose in jets and spouts,
and the hummer follows the water,
loops and soars, turns and hovers, leaps.
I shorten the arc toward myself,

and the hummer comes to my hands.
It enters the fine spray; it flies in the spray.
It alights on the tomato cage, and waits,
raises a wing, gets a squirt in one armpit,
and the other armpit. It shows its butt
and wiggles its tail. What's that gold thread?
The hummer is spraying me back.

There's a yellow bird that is barely anything
but a reed, a tube of song.
Its beak opens as wide as its throat, its body,
which trembles through and through.
It's a yellow-feathered skinbag of song,
and it sings all day.

The next day dawns.
I am at: the exact Real, and I myself am real,
bare feet and hands, feet on the floor,
hands writing, one holding the pen cap, the other
the pen. Walking and writing,
I look at, then away from the sun, higher and higher
warmth on my face.
A strand of web moves, runs, shines like an EEG line.
Palm fronds blow.
Windy day—all the natural things are blowing.
The man-made things are still but
for cars going their own ways.
Their grilles are solid smiles.
At the exact Real, myself real/true,
I am a smiling being.
              a 3-line smile:

At my parents' rolltop desk (mine now)—neater than it's ever been
in their lives. 2 drawers empty—all the pigeonholes nice and neat.

Each of us kids had for ourself a pigeonhole or a drawer or a space. In the knee well, a box of toys that belonged to all. This desk housed 8. I ringed a haku lei around the shade of the pink lamp, which used to sit on their nightstand. The photos are of my beloved people when they were young. Woodblock prints from Hanoi—6 for a few dollars—Vietnamese have Monkey too. The clock ticks and ticks and ticks... Cold. Hungry. Go out in the sun amongst the Santa Barbara daisies. I'm trying not to roll on my rolling chair down the slope of this floor.

Stop to appreciate actions, business done:
Made the phone calls.
The check <u>did</u> come in the mail.

I know how to turn anything into worry on a to-do list. Fret. Fret. Fret. Fret.

At the hump of my back—the burden hump—the *chi* is stuck—like swallowing egg too fast.

The Chinese made list poems.

Enjoy my new Hanuman and Shiva lunch box. Hanuman Monkey wears a bell on his tail. Stay awake. Hanuman was a military general. I have misplaced two mindfulness belts, just when I'm learning not to lose glasses and keys so often.

On the bulletin board beside our desk:

—The little boy jumps into the waves with open arms.
—The sandhill crane jumps with wings lifted.
    All the cranes, and the boy, are facing west.
—Joseph and guitar with audience member. For
        my son:
            joy in art
            good times
            music ~ beautiful timing
            people who love to hear him

Two yellow and black butterflies are dancing up and up toward the sun.

I go outdoors, and I go indoors, hew chunks of time-for-poems. Under the ticking clock. The White Rabbit is looking at the clock. Beside the telephone. I have to phone. I have to FAX bio-biblio info.

On the wall: My mother embroidered my father's calligraphy:

Beyond mountains, yet mountains.
Across seas, yet seas.

⌐   ⌐   ⌐

Now the bird is saying Come here. Come here.
The pocket knife I gave my father, and the pen—returned to me.
They—my mother and my father—sat at this desk for fifty years
each. The way they sat—they had been entirely here. They sat square
in this chair. They concentrated. They wrote carefully, lovingly form-
ing each stroke of each word. They rewrote for the beauty of the hand-
writing. They did not need to clear a space; they wrote at the edge of
the fish tank. Order was within them, and emanated from them.

Only write what I care to.

March 23—In my office at school
    I am out on my 4th-floor balcony.
    If it were not for poetry,
    I wouldn't've unjammed the doors,
    and be standing amongst the rooftops.
    Green hills surround me and the green
    copper eaves. A green copper pineapple
    caps the Library—Welcome. Welcome.
    Down through an immense copper-framed skylight,
    I can see a bookroom where I've never been.
    The Campanile bongs and echoes into my nook.
    I have been here a long time. Since I was young.
    And the nearest buildings and the biggest trees,
    the oldest trees also here long ago.
    In the hills, away from the trees, are the recent blocking
        cement structures—probably labs.
    Sounds of planes and air conditioning.
    Breezes touch me.

Clanging of dropped sewerpipes.
I should feel nostalgia for times gone but
I have this vista. This vista is my own.
     This place mine for staying till old.

March 24 Friday
     I will try three days with the attitude that I can control
          (my sense of) Time.
     I'll read the morning paper in the morning, despite
          bad news.
     I'll volunteer to cook lunch.
     I'll wait and watch the water heat up instead of going off
          to do something else.
     I'll spontaneously return phone calls without premedita-
          tion for days.
     I'll try not looking forward to the next meal, the next
          course.
     "As soon as I get this over with, I'll start to live."

March 25 Saturday—I hardly tried poetry yesterday—knocked
out by the longbook, which refuses to end. Months ago, two
mornings, I awoke feeling: The longbook is over. But it keeps
coming to me, and I keep writing it. "Over the river, more rivers
/ Over the mountain, more mountains." But my father had been
happy singing that poem, and my mother illustrated it with
birds in the trees and flowers, and birds in the water, and a drag-
on and a phoenix in the sky. Joy, and more joy. My father
explained, "Learn, and learn more. Always more to learn."
Infinities of wonders to learn. He did not mean trudging and
drudging across continents.

March 26   The Poet's day:
     Wander through the day, choose (among treasured
     things), and wrap a gift, and give it away.
     Sit and jot.
     Wash the dishes after every meal and snack.

Run errands and know you are running errands.
Buy cheap beautiful notebooks.
Sit and jot some more.
Use each fountain pen.
Do not be so afraid.

March 27   I am 59 years and 5 months old, on an airplane. I can write prose on plane rides, and in the car as Earll drives. Engines—inertia takes over the body—do not allow me tides. (Feelings come and feelings go, leave and return like the tide. And the words are like tide lines.) The flow and wash have stopped. I need to arrive and settle in. Gary Snyder's advice: Stay put. Yes the happy life is one in which I get to stay home.

Approaching her 60th birthday—and desiring respite from The Fifth Book of Peace, *the "longbook" she had been working on for more than a decade—acclaimed novelist Maxine Hong Kingston decided she would switch to poetry, a pursuit she came by naturally. "I spoke poetry and sang it before I learned to read and write," she recalls.*

Her father, Tom Hong, who left China in 1924, had been a scholar and teacher in a small village near Canton. In Stockton, California, where Kingston was born in 1940, he worked in a gambling house—but, Kingston says, "my father had memorized classical Chinese poetry and Confucius, and he would go around reciting that." Her mother, Ying Lan Hong, who had trained as a midwife in Canton, came from a long tradition of public storytellers. Kingston can recall her mother holding her out the window to greet her arriving grandfathers: "She'd say, 'Sing for your grandfathers and make up a poem for them and make up a song.'"

Kingston was her parents' third child, and the first of six who would be born in America. Her first book, The Woman Warrior *(1976), was drawn from her mother's "talk stories" of her ancestors. Blending legend with autobiographical elements of her Chinese immigrant experience, the memoir established Kingston as a powerful voice in literature and an outspoken advocate for social change.*

In To Be the Poet—*from which "I Call on the Muses of Poetry…" is drawn—Kingston ranges from ruminations on her travels and family to commentary on her adoption of the poet's life and advice from fellow writers and mentors about her quest. With her mother's hands squeezing her waist at the window, Kingston remembers, the poems and songs had simply emerged without effort: "Now that I'm past 60, I want art to give me that delight of being a child again."*

Jane Juska

A Round-Heeled Woman

I stood at the corner of College and Ashby, one of the busiest inter-
sections of Berkeley, and listened intently to my friend Sandy. I
love this corner. Almost always it is crowded with people walking
and talking, young and old, homeless and not. It is a university corner and has a vitality I find in no other city, with the possible excep-
tions of Florence, Oxford, Ann Arbor, Cambridge, and I could go on.
Be patient while I outgrow an adolescent addiction to hyperbole.

Thanksgiving, not far away, will empty Berkeley of many of its
young—about thirty thousand—but now, the air sang with the energy of people of all ages busy with ideas and each other. I stepped back
from the curb as an old BMW roared around the corner, heedless of
those who might be waiting to cross. Always interesting, Berkeley is
not always friendly.

Sandy's voice, its Chicago accent outperforming all the noises of the street, says, "This Jonah guy's coming when? This weekend? You've got to be kidding me!" I smile shyly. Sandy says, "Condoms! Have you got condoms?" A passing couple looks at us and smiles. I put my head down and my hand up to one side of my face. "You don't!" Sandy yells. "Your generation never thinks of things like that. That's why I'm talking to you." Today, Sandy looks like Margaret O'Brien in *Meet Me in St. Louis* dressed for Halloween. Sandy's clothes are big, long, wide on her slim little body. The top is green, the pants some shade of magenta. The sleeves fall over her wrists, the hems of her pants cover her shoes. Even without the voice, Sandy is someone people notice. The more excited she gets, the more she flaps. She is a sail whose sheets no one can catch. She is three sheets to the wind without a need for alcohol to put her there.

"Let's have a cup of tea." I point at the café across the street. I am regretting sharing my joyful secret. But I had to. Keeping the deliciousness all to myself was more than I could manage. As the days passed since I had answered the first letters, tension had mounted. Sometimes, inside my own silence, I felt terror and desire wrapped in a ball, starting somewhere in my middle, rising into my chest, then dropping suddenly to the parts of me I wasn't used to feeling at all. It might really happen, a man might really touch me. Sometimes, I thought I might faint. So I had told a few friends, one of them Sandy, this young woman with the pink-tipped hair.

Sandy is on a roll. She throws her hands into the air. Birds dart away. "My generation? Condoms are just part of everyday life. They're de rigueur. We wouldn't think of having sex without some kind of protection." She softens and puts her hands on my shoulder. "But sweetie, I know. I know guys your age, they go way back, they go back to the time when they didn't use anything, or if they did, it was the girl who was supposed to provide the protection, a diaphragm, something like that. STDs? Never heard of 'em." I refrain from lecturing her on syphilis and the generations it had ravaged before penicillin. Let her rant. It is too late to stop her or the people who slow to hear her. I hear titters.

Sandy and I met at a nearby exercise studio where we are regulars. Like her, I am a fervent exerciser. Now. Not always. In the past I had subscribed to Mark Twain's "Whenever I feel the urge to exercise, I lie down until it passes." And so I grew fat.

In 1983, I turned fifty. I weighed 234 pounds. My son was a runaway living on the streets of Berkeley. I was polishing off a goodly amount of scotch each evening. I was living in a house I couldn't afford, and I was working sixty hours a week. I had not had sex in fifteen years, save with myself, an act grown increasingly unappealing with each ten pounds I added to my five-foot-three-inch frame. Paradoxically, I was a successful teacher of English in a California public high school. I was good at one thing. I was a helluva teacher. Teaching saved me from becoming a full-time drunk but not from becoming an obese, middle-aged, unhappy, distraught, frantic woman. I was bound for an early death.

At my fiftieth birthday party, one of my friends—in what surely he meant as a friendly, not a hostile, gesture—took many photographs of the people gathered to celebrate this important birthday, of the lavish buffet, the fully stocked bar, the hors d'oeuvres, the gifts, and of me. What he did was a kind of intervention. Nobody knew how to tell me I was out of control. So Rob did this: he put those photographs, carefully selected so that I was in every one of them, into an album, and a few days later, he gave the album to me. There I was, multiple images of me on every single page for pages and pages. Dreadful, absolutely dreadful. My color was high, like my blood pressure, which is to say, my cheeks were flushed; my chins rolled over the collar of my dress. (Yes, I had found a dress at the store for large women, which is where I shopped when absolute necessity made me do it; otherwise, I went to school to teach in one of three muumuus a friend had run up on her sewing machine.) My front self stuck out, way out, my breasts were enormous of course—surely you know by now—and I looked awful. So I never looked anywhere that might show my reflection—not in a mirror, not into a store window, and never into the faces of people I saw coming toward me on the street; their quick glances, their quicker turning away, telling me everything I did not want to know.

Still, public humiliations were there to remind me. One day, I took my son, then about seven, to the little train up in Tilden Park. The little train is a miniature train in which kids and their parents may ride

along a miniature track through the leafiness of the park. My son and
I sat in one of the cars, my bulk overflowing its sides. Behind us sat a
child who could talk and sing and who did. About me. "Lady, lady,"
he chanted singsong over and over, "fat old lady." It was the longest
ride of my life. My son laughed—what else could he do? I was devas-
tated. When I got the courage to face the facts of my obesity, I would
realize that, in the four years since leaving my husband, I had gained
seventy pounds. I was safe from men, to be sure, but not from children and other living things.

I was also not safe from illness. In my forties I began to get sick
every so often and then regularly. At least once a year, during the
Christmas holidays usually, I could count on a severe bronchitis at-
tacking my lungs and staying there for months. I lost time from school,
went to school sick, and was exhausted well into spring. I continued to
smoke. When school ended in June, and I was able to force myself to
look back on my year, I had to admit that it had been lousy: half of it
I had spent dragging myself to school, half of it getting ready to drag
myself there. And I am not accounting here—you can figure this out
for yourself—for the quality of my mothering.

Then came the year the bronchitis turned into pneumonia. I coughed
blood and I got scared. So, put it all together—my health, my appearance, my all-too-soon-to-be-orphaned son—and I changed my life.

At Alta Bates Hospital in Berkeley, with the help of a nutritionist,
a psychologist, an exercise physiologist, many aerobics teachers—
every one of them heroic, every one of them memorable—I lost
weight, one hundred pounds of it. My goals were three: (1) run the
Bay to Breakers (seven miles through San Francisco to the Pacific
Ocean, a hundred thousand people dressed in serious running shorts,
dressed in costumes to shock and amuse, or dressed in nothing at all;
(2) fit into 501 Levi's; and (3) go to the Black and White Ball (a benefit for the symphony in the middle of San Francisco, when all of the
Civic Center—the enormous plaza bordered by the opera house, the
symphony hall, City Hall, the library—becomes a dance floor where
jazz bands and polka bands and rock bands and the San Francisco
Symphony play music while men in black and white tuxedos and
women in black and white ball gowns dance into the wee hours of the

morning). It is the most romantic event in the city. In May I ran my first Bay to Breakers, and I ran three after that. I am wearing 501's as I write this. The ball? Two out of three's not bad.

One year later, in March 1984, I weighed 122 pounds. On my fifty-first birthday, a friend took pictures of me. I looked awful: no color, scrawny, caved in everywhere. So I put back some. More or less, I've kept the weight off, though not without the help of Diet Center, Weight Watchers, and my own fear of being fat.

At the center of all this obsessiveness was the exercise studio. I was like Ben in *Death of a Salesman,* who boasted, "I went into the jungle and when I came out—by God—I was rich!" Me? I went into the gym and when I came out—by God—I was thin! You can never be too rich or too thin, right? Wrong. You can be either or both. But I have yet to meet a woman who thinks she's just right. Anyway, here's the gym:

In the eighties high-impact aerobic exercise was all the rage, even among serious-minded students of exercise and its benefits. Coaches at the university began requiring some of their athletes to enroll in aerobics classes as a way to develop balance and coordination. Physicians and counselors of addicts recommended aerobic exercise as a substitute for addiction, as a way to get high without benefit of illegal substances. Classes were full. Newspapers carried stories of exercisers who turned violent when someone took their space on the floor.

When I entered the studio for the very first time, at 234 pounds, dressed in the only exercise clothes that would fit—sweatpants and sweatshirt—one of the instructors barred the way to the floor. "Hi," she said, her smile chock-full of teeth, "I'm Debi. And I'm sorry, but we'll have to see your doctor's written permission before you can take classes here."

She was little and cute, bouncy as all get-out, perky even. She was no match for my girth. I swept her aside and walked to the middle of the floor. "Start the music," I ordered. She did.

On my way home from the studio, I stopped at an athletic-shoe store. Inside, a young man asked me if he could help. "I want a pair of running shoes," I said. "For whom?" he inquired. (Salespersons in Berkeley talk like that.) "For me," I said. He looked doubtful. "How often do you plan to run?" he asked. "Every day." The look on his face said, Humor her, she'll be dead in a week.

But I wasn't. I began to run from mailbox to mailbox. In the beginning weeks, I made it to the second mailbox. Before long, I wasn't counting mailboxes anymore, and not long after that, I began to run races. Uphill, downhill, far and near.

I discovered my body. It stretched, it bent, it bowed, it jumped and jiggled and reached and stepped and moved—to rhythm, to the commands—"Suck it in! Breathe! Pull it in! Inhale! Exhale!" I came alive.

One evening I found myself in the front row of the studio, only inches from the mirror that covered the entire front wall, the only place left on the crowded floor. Usually, I got to class early to claim my spot in the back row. This particular evening—I went to class after school so was sometimes late—I found myself next to a gigantic young man who could only be a linebacker. On my other side was a tall young man, well over six feet, heavily muscled, whom I had noticed before, who seemed to spend most of his day at the studio, taking two, three, and more aerobics classes. Later, I learned from one of the instructors that he had been sent by his drug counselor, that he was sweating out drugs and alcohol and using his time in a way that would keep him out of the hospital and out of jail. In between classes, outside, at the curb, he smoked furiously, one cigarette after another.

"It's Raining Men" roared through the studio, and we began to move to its insistent beat. On my left, the man's long blond hair swung from side to side as the music pumped its way into our bodies. On the other side of me the linebacker pounded his legs into the floor. For a brief moment, I feared I might be crushed between them. Then we caught the rhythm—"Back two, three, four; up two, three, four; pick up those knees!" I looked at the three of us in the mirror, waving our hands, raising our knees, and I knew that at age fifty-two, I could keep up with these boys who were no more than twenty. We grinned at each other in the mirror as the sweat streamed down our faces, and congratulated ourselves silently when the Weather Girls brought things to an end with "Hallelujah" and "Amen."

Eventually, the young men disappeared; I stayed on and am there to this day. High-impact aerobics was followed by low-impact, safer for the joints. Things calmed down at the studio. Now, the regulars meet at 6:45 in the morning to exchange a bit of talk and to sweat against the coming of the new day. The times are different; people have calmed down; the energy is underground; the world seems to have grown up, not an altogether felicitous change. Given the seriousness—nay, the humorlessness—of the new century, I find Sandy especially precious.

"What about oral sex?" Sandy peers intently through her green-rimmed harlequin glasses, the scarlet spikes of her hair piercing the early morning fog. "Are you listening, Jane?" Now the passersby have definitely slowed. A crowd is about to gather. "AIDS," Sandy shouts. She is impatient, like a teacher who has had to ask the same question too many times. "Can you get AIDS from oral sex? Do you know, Jane?" She reins herself in and says, as if speaking to a slow-minded child, "Do you plan on having oral sex?" Her patience is at an end. "Oral sex, are you going to do it or not?" A woman smiles as she passes. She nods yes.

"Listen," says Sandy, "I've got to go. I'm due at my therapist." She hugs me. "Don't worry. You'll do fine. Me, I'm crazy, I know it, everybody knows it. Don't listen to me." And then, from the middle of the street, which she is crossing against the light, she turns and calls to me, "Call the San Francisco Hotline. Promise me!" I nod fervently, eager to do whatever I can to get Sandy out of traffic.

I hurry home to call the San Francisco Hotline. Because, of course, I plan on having oral sex. At least, I hope I will have oral sex. And I plan on giving some. In the dimness of my memory, I am good at both.

The young man on the other end of the hotline has a gentle, soothing voice. The possibility of contracting AIDS from oral sex is higher than had been thought in earlier times. My heart sinks. But the percentage is still low: up from 3 to perhaps 8 percent of the time the disease is contracted by way of oral sex. There should be little to fear, he tells me, as long as there are no cuts or sores on either the genital area or in the mouth. Of course, there won't be. The young man advises me that, if I do not know my partner intimately, I will do well to ask him for his sexual history. Okay, I will do whatever anybody tells me to. I will write Jonah at once. I will ask him, casually—good lord, how would that go: "Oh and by the way, I was just wondering, uh…" Jonah—this stranger—will be here within a week.

🌸 *Jane Juska lived a lifetime before authoring her first book,* A Round-Heeled Woman: My Late-Life Adventures in Love and Romance. *The ribald story candidly chronicles her late-life sex romps, detailing the circumstances that prompted her to place the following ad in* The New York Review of Books *in 1999: "Before I turn 67—next March—I would like to have a lot of sex with a man I like. If you want to talk first, Trollope works for me."*

Born in 1933 and the survivor of a "Puritanical small-town Ohio childhood," Juska moved to the San Francisco Bay area in the 1950s and became a high school English teacher. Divorced in 1972 and consumed with the challenges of raising a young son with whom she had a troubled relationship, Juska gradually neglected herself. At age 50, severely overweight and facing looming health crises, she resolved to reclaim her life. Years of dieting, exercise, and psychoanalysis eventually restored her to physical and mental health.

Throughout this time, teaching was Juska's passion—and her salvation. In addition to her high school duties, she contributed several articles on teaching to educational journals and taught English to prison inmates. Despite taking up a number of activities when she left teaching—a writing group, volunteer work, choral singing—Juska says she "just wasn't tired enough" to retire. Perhaps this restlessness led her to place that incendiary ad. That and a craving for human touch that she had ignored for more than 10 years.

As related in Juska's follow-up memoir, Unaccompanied Women: Late-Life Adventures in Love, Sex, and Real Estate *(2006), the high-energy septuagenarian continues to pursue her quest for a man: not a husband or even a partner—just the perfect lover, once described by Katharine Hepburn as one who "lives nearby and visits often."*

Julia Alvarez

A Cafecito Story

J oe buys a parcel next to Miguel's. They make a pact. They will not rent their plots to the compañía and cut down their trees. They will keep to the old ways. They will provide a better coffee.

And, Joe adds, you will learn your letters. I myself will teach you.

Every day, under Miguel's gentle direction, Joe learns how to grow coffee. They make terraces and plant trees.

Every night, under the light of an oil lamp, Miguel and his family learn their ABCs. They write letters and learn words.

BY THE TIME Miguel and Carmen and their children have learned to write their names, the little seeds have sprouted. When the trees are a foot high, the family has struggled through a sentence. All of them can read a page by the time the trees reach up to Miguel's knees. When the coffee is as tall as little Miguelina, they have progressed to chapters. In three years, by the time of the first coffee harvest from trees Joe has planted, Miguel and Carmen and their children can read a whole book.

It is amazing how much better coffee grows when sung to by birds or when through an opened window comes the sound of a human voice reading words on paper that still holds the memory of the tree it used to be.

MIGUEL AND JOE'S IDEA SPREADS. Many of the small farmers join them, banding together into a cooperativo and building their own beneficio for processing the beans rather than having to pay high fees to use the compañía facilities. They can now read the contracts the buyers bring and argue for better terms. Joe buys books in the ciudad where he goes periodically to ship the cooperativo coffee to the United States. Carmen cooks for the workers and adds eggs from her hens or cheese from her goats to the bowl of víveres she serves her family at night. More hens and more goats mean more abono for the coffee plants. Miguelina no longer makes a zero when she is asked to write her name.

The years go by. The hillsides are full of songbirds, the cedros are tall and elegant, the guama trees full, the cherries bright red, and the hair on Joe's head is turning white, which is natural when you are fifty-five.

FOR HIS FIFTY-FIFTH CHRISTMAS, Joe decides to visit Nebraska. Over the years, his brothers and sisters and their children have visited the farm-cooperativo, but Joe has never gone back.

Superintendent would boil me alive in a vat of coffee, he jokes when his sister suggests a visit. Remember, I left that teaching job mid-year.

Don't worry, his sister tells him. When you called mid-year, saying you wouldn't be back, the super was only too glad to get rid of a young radical.

I was a young radical? Joe asks.

In Nebraska you were. After all, you liked reading more than football. Oh, please come, Joey, his sister adds. I hate the thought of you all alone at Christmas without your family.

I have a family, Joe explains. Although he has never married, he has become a husband to the land. He is surrounded by his large campesino familia, all of whom he has taught to read and write.

But still, a man needs to go back to where he started from and take a look around.

Julia Alvarez calls A Cafecito Story *(2001) a "green fable" with its genesis in real life.*

In 1996, Alvarez and her husband, ophthalmologist Bill Eichner (who had grown up farming in Nebraska), started an organic coffee farm in her parents' native land, the Dominican Republic. Called Alta Gracia, the farm adheres to the principles of the Fair Trade movement: The coffee is grown using sustainable agricultural methods, and the farmers receive a fair price for their beans. The couple also built a school on the site to teach basic reading and writing. When they took a bilingual edition of the book to the farm, Alvarez says, "One of the special moments of my writing life happened… our once-illiterate neighbors were able to read passages in which their names appeared!"

The second of her parents' four daughters, Alvarez was born in New York City in 1950 but moved back to the Dominican Republic with her family when she was three months old. Alvarez spent her formative years in the DR, surrounded by an enormous extended family. When she was 10, her parents were forced to flee the Trujillo dictatorship. Alvarez was uprooted, then transplanted to a cramped apartment in New York. "We came to this country and here I became one of the others. So maybe that made me develop a certain sensitivity," Alvarez has said of her desire to become a writer.

Alvarez graduated summa cum laude *from Middlebury College in 1971, then earned a master's degree in creative writing from Syracuse University in 1975. She and Eichner married in 1989. When they are not growing or harvesting coffee beans on Alta Gracia, the couple lives on an 11-acre farm in Vermont's Champlain Valley. "I am a Dominican, hyphen, American," observes Alvarez. "As a fiction writer, I find that the most exciting things happen in the realm of that hyphen—the place where two worlds collide or blend together."*

Anne Tyler

Back When
We Were Grownups

"As soon as I sort my belongings I'm moving to a retirement home," Rebecca's mother said. "I already know which one. It's just that I need to get my belongings sorted first."

They were sitting in Rebecca's mother's living room—Rebecca in an armchair, her mother on the couch. Her mother wore her usual outfit of pastel polyester top and dark, skinny knit slacks with the creases stitched down the front. She was eighty-seven years old—a little cornhusk doll, straw-colored and drily rustling. Rebecca had outweighed her since late childhood, but she had always considered her to be a sturdy woman. It came as a shock to picture her in a retirement home. "What's made you think of moving?" she asked. "Are you having any health problems?"

"No, not a one. But Church Valley isn't like when you lived here, Rebecca. After they built that mall out where the duck farm used to be, why, seems we just got hollow at the center. Downtown isn't even downtown anymore. So I signed up for a unit at Havenhurst, but I don't know when I'll get to go there with all these belongings to sort."

Rebecca glanced around her. She didn't see any evidence that her mother had started yet. Not that there was much to do—this was a small house, fastidiously tidy—but every object had the glued-down appearance of something that had stayed in the same position for decades. Two hurricane lamps were spaced symmetrically on the mantel, an Oriental vase was centered in the front window, and the table at Rebecca's elbow bore a shrinelike arrangement of three gilt-framed photos, a candy dish, and a bowl of faded silk flowers. If she were to pick up, say, her parents' wedding photo and set it down again, she knew her mother would be over in two seconds to readjust its location by a fraction of an inch.

"Maybe I could help," she said.

"Oh, no, thank you," her mother said. "I won't forget what happened when your Aunt Ida tried to help. It took me days to undo what she'd done! And some things I could never undo. For instance, she threw away an entire sheet of postage stamps; three-cent postage stamps. I wasn't aware of it at the time because I was out of the room, fixing her a snack. That's how it is when people try to help: they need snacks and cups of tea, and before you know it you've gone to more trouble than if they'd stayed at home. I brought out a plate of those peppermint patties that she's always been so fond of, and then she told me she was on a diet. I said, 'What do you mean, a diet? I've been nagging you all your life to diet and it didn't do the least bit of good; so why would you take it into your head now that you're in your eighties?' And Ida said—"

"But the stamps..." Rebecca prodded her. Then she wondered why she'd bothered, since even the stamps were not the point of the conversation.

"The thing is, I didn't know she'd thrown them out. There I was in the kitchen, waiting on her hand and foot, and meanwhile Ida was in the living room merrily discarding my stamps. When I went to look for them later in the week, I couldn't find them. I phoned her. I said, 'Ida, what did you do with those stamps?' 'What stamps?' she asked, innocent as an angel. 'That sheet of stamps in my desk drawer,' I said. 'There's not a thing in that drawer now but dried-up ballpoint pens with advertising on them.' And Ida said, 'I hope I didn't throw them away.' 'Throw them away!' I told her.

Rebecca said, "Well, luckily they were—"

"I said, 'Where did you throw them away?' and she said, 'Now I'm not saying for certain that I did, you understand.' 'Where?' I said, and she said, 'The recycling sack under the sink, maybe?' I said, 'No.' I said,

'You didn't.' I said, 'You couldn't have.' Because I'd gotten rid of that sack on paper collection day."

"Luckily," Rebecca said, "they were only three-cent stamps."

"A *hundred* three-cent stamps, might I add. What we're saying is, my sister threw away three dollars. And I told her as much. 'Fine, I'll pay you back,' she said. 'Next time I come over to visit, I'll bring three dollar bills.' Which is so exactly like her, isn't it? I said, 'Now, what on earth will that accomplish? You'd still have wasted three dollars, and all for nothing. We might as well have burned it; that money's simply gone. Turned to paper soup in the recycling plant.'"

Rebecca started jiggling one foot.

"So I'll just do my sorting on my own," her mother told her. "Never let it be said that I'm unable to learn from experience."

And she tucked her chin in modestly and gazed down at her lap, while Rebecca recrossed her legs and started jiggling the other foot.

IT HAD TAKEN her more than a month to find the time for this trip, and now they were in the full bloom of summer—a Thursday in mid-July. When they set out on a walk to Ida's after lunch, the town appeared to be liquefied by the heat, all wavery and smeared like something behind antique window glass. The clay path leading down to the river was baked as hard as linoleum, and the footbridge's black metal railing burned Rebecca's hand. The river itself—wide but shallow, pebble-bottomed— seemed sluggish and exhausted, its sound less a rush than a series of slow glugs. Rebecca paused halfway across to study it. "The funniest thing," she told her mother. "Lately, I've started loving rivers."

"Loving them!"

"I've always *liked* them, of course; but I look at a river now and it just satisfies my eyes, you know? It seems to me so… old-fashioned."

"Maybe you should move back here, then."

"Well…"

"Why not? The girls are grown; you've got no responsibilities."

"Only the Open Arms," Rebecca said.

"The what? Oh, the Open Arms. Well, that's the Davitches' business; not yours."

"No, actually, it's mine," Rebecca said. This was a startling thought, for some reason. She said, "It's how I make my money, what little of it there is. How would I make any money in Church Valley?"

"I'm sure you'd find something or other," her mother said.

"Besides, I've got Poppy to think of."

"Poppy! Is that old man still alive?"

"Of course he's still alive. Next December he'll be a hundred. I'm planning a gigantic hundredth-birthday party for him," Rebecca said. Then she stopped to reflect upon the oddly boastful note that seemed to have crept into her voice.

"What I'd do," her mother said, as if Rebecca hadn't spoken, "is put my house in your name instead of selling it. Let you move right in. Leave you most of the furnishings, even."

Rebecca said, "Oh, I suspect you'll need to sell your house in order to afford the retirement home."

"I'm not getting but a little studio unit. The least expensive model. I can pay for it out of my pension."

She had worked for nearly thirty years in the basement of the county courthouse, keeping track of old documents. Rebecca didn't suppose that her pension was very large. She said gently, "Thanks anyhow, Mother."

But as they climbed the steep path on the other side of the river, approaching her aunt's part of town, she briefly entertained a fantasy of returning here to live. She imagined her routine: each day crossing the river for her meager supply of groceries, stopping first at the library the way she used to as a child. She had been the kind of child a librarian would love, she saw now, so pale and polite and considerate, careful to check that her hands were spotless before reverently selecting yet another Louisa May Alcott book. This was in the late fifties, when other children were turning to TV, but Rebecca—pudgy even then and stodgily dressed, her father dead and her mother several years older than any of her classmates' mothers—was not in step with most other children. She had always been the town's Bright Girl. ("Brain" was the term they used.) She tended to stay on the fringe of things, observing from a distance, and she had noticed that what she observed was often outside the normal frame of vision. It was as if she didn't *have* a frame of vision, so that during the Christmas pageant her attention might be caught by some small personal drama in the audience while everybody else was watching the stage. But she was not unhappy. She had had several friends, and in high school she'd had a boyfriend. And she was good at amusing herself when she was alone. In fact she'd been very content with things just the way they were; her set-apart position had felt comfortable, and restful.

When she grew up and left for college, the librarian gave her a going-away gift: a leather-bound blank book entitled *A Reader's Life List.* But Rebecca used only the first few pages, because college was when everything changed.

College was when she met Joe.

She said, "I don't suppose Miss Bolt still works at the library, does she?"

"Good heavens," her mother said, "I haven't thought of Miss Bolt in ages. I'm sure she must have passed on. Anyway, now they use volunteers, and the library isn't open but three half-days a week."

It was ludicrous to imagine moving back here. Rebecca didn't know a soul.

But when she pointed that out—"See there? To me Church Valley's all strangers"—her mother said, "Oh, piffle. You know Aunt Ida. You know the Finches. And Abbie Field and Sherry and the Nolan twins."

"Do you still see all of them?"

"Well, of course! This town is very close-knit."

She must mean the older people in town, though, for it was clear that she didn't recognize the various teenagers and young mothers they met walking along Grove Street. She threaded her way between them without so much as a glance; and for all the attention they paid her, she might have been invisible.

Aunt Ida lived above Gates Drugstore. Arnold Gates, the pharmacist, had been her husband, and after his death she'd sold the drugstore but arranged to continue living in the four little rooms upstairs. Nobody would have guessed she was Rebecca's mother's sister. She tended to put on a little weight, and she dyed her hair a metallic red, and she wore frilly, too-young dresses and bright makeup. Today she was all in pink—pink strappy sandals and pink toenails, even—with some kind of gauzy pink ruching knotted around her throat. And her apartment was as cluttered as her clothing. "Now, let me clear you a path," she said as they entered. "Oh, my, what is this doing here?"—referring to a Raggedy Ann doll grinning from the carpet. A reasonable question, since Ida had no children or grandchildren. (The great tragedy of her life, she always said.) But then, she was forever opening her doors to other people's offspring.

When Rebecca was a very small girl, she had nourished a secret day-dream that her parents would painlessly die and she could go live with her aunt. Ida was so welcoming and easygoing; her household seemed capable of limitless expansion, and almost any time Rebecca dropped in she found somebody staying a week or two—a toddler whose mother was sick, or Arnold Gates's ne'er-do-well nephew, or, on one memorable occasion, three members of a Polish wrestling team visiting Church Valley High on some kind of sports exchange program. When Rebecca's father actually did die (felled by a stroke just after her ninth birthday), she had felt so guilty that she'd avoided her aunt for months. And besides, her mother needed her at home.

"Well, come on in where I can look at you," Ida was saying. "Oh, my! I would never have the courage to wear plaid with paisley, but on you it's so artistic."

Rebecca's mother, moving an armload of magazines so she could set-tle in a rocker, said, "You didn't tell me they were painting the hardware store, Ida. We passed it and it just about hit me in the face. Oxblood, I would call it; or, no, more like magenta. I said to Rebecca, I said, 'What a pushy color!' And then of course the Woolworth's; Rebecca's not been here since they closed the Woolworth's, and I can't even remember the store that used to be next to it, can you? I was trying to think. Not the jeweler's; that was across the street. Not the pet supply. Well, I know it will come to me eventually. Wait! No, not the shoe repair…"

"Sit right here; move the cat," Ida told Rebecca. "Look at what I've made you! Froot Loop Bark Candy, it's called. I got the recipe out of the paper. Isn't it pretty? The bright spots come from the Froot Loops and the lighter spots are colored-marshmallow bits. I tried them out first on the neighbors' little boy; he was staying here a while because, oh, it's such a sad story…"

"A fingernail place!" Rebecca's mother said. "That's what it was! Can you imagine a place devoted to nothing but fingernails? No wonder it closed!"

Rebecca took a bite from her piece of candy, which looked more like some kind of novelty toilet soap. As soon as she could get her teeth unstuck, she asked her aunt, "Is that Percival?"

She meant the cat—a fat gray tabby. "Why, no, dear," Ida said, "that's Daisy. Percival died last Christmastime."

"Oh, I'm sorry to hear it."

"Yes, I had to have him put to sleep on account of kidney trouble. I wanted Dr. More to do it before he retired; you know he'd tended Percival ever since kittenhood."

"I myself," Rebecca's mother said, "have never had a professional manicure in my life and I don't believe my nails are any the worse for it. Who knows what you could pick up in such a place? Sharing instruments with strangers—files and clippers and scissors and such."

"Dr. More retired at the end of the year when he turned sixty-five," Ida told Rebecca. "He said he was moving to Florida."

"Well, he should know," Rebecca's mother said smartly.

There was a sudden silence, as if the sisters had surprised themselves with this momentary convergence in their conversation. Then Ida sat forward, clasping her plump, ringed hands, and said, "How long will you be with us, Rebecca?"

"Just until tomorrow. I've left Poppy with Zeb overnight, but I should be back in time to give him lunch."

"And tell us about NoNo! I'm so thrilled that she's engaged."

This was what Rebecca loved about her aunt. Her mother had not inquired after NoNo, or Patch or Biddy either; they weren't blood relations. Her only question had concerned her "real" granddaughter, Min Foo—how her pregnancy was proceeding—and she had worn a pinched and remote expression as she asked, because she had disapproved of Min Foo ever since her second marriage, the one to LaVon. But Ida seemed equally attached to all four girls, and still sent each of them a dollar bill in a Hallmark card for their birthdays. "Your mother says NoNo isn't planning much of a wedding," she said now, "but I hope she'll change her mind. Is she thinking she's too old? She's not too old! Nowadays lots of people don't get married till their forties. And she's waited so long for Mr. Right; all the more reason to celebrate."

"Oh, she's celebrating, for sure," Rebecca said. "Along with you two, I trust," she added, sending them each a glance. Ida beamed and nodded. Rebecca's mother gazed thoughtfully at a rainbow afghan on the floor. "What she means is, she doesn't want anything formal. And that's partly because of her age but more, I think, because Barry's been married before."

"Well, what has that got to do with the price of eggs in China?" Ida asked.

"Tea," Rebecca's mother said.

"What?"

"*Tea* in China."

"The bride is the one who counts," Ida said. "You tell her so, Rebecca. Tell her to have a long white dress, a veil—the works. Flower girls, attendants... Tell her Barry should have a best man. Maybe his son, if he's old enough. Is he old enough?"

"He's twelve."

"That's plenty old enough!"

"Well, maybe," Rebecca said. "He's kind of a young twelve, though."

"How does he get along with NoNo?"

"All right, I guess. It's hard to say. He's very quiet. At our Fourth of July barbeque, he just sat in a corner and read a book."

"Well he's going to love you-all once he gets to know you," Ida said.

She passed the candy again, but this time Rebecca and her mother both refused. Ida herself was the only one who took a second piece. "Law," she said, licking each finger daintily, "it seems like yesterday we three were planning *your* wedding! You made the prettiest bride."

"Well. I certainly had a pretty dress," Rebecca said, because the dress had been sewn by her mother and Ida, working almost around the clock. (She'd given them two weeks' notice.)

"We took down all your measurements and then you lost eight pounds, remember? We got to Baltimore the day of the wedding and found you just a shadow of your former self. Right up till time for the ceremony we had to baste and pin and tuck... You'd turned into a skeleton! I guess it was bridal jitters."

Rebecca had been nowhere near a skeleton; just slightly less fat than usual. And that was due to pure happiness, not to jitters. She had been so extravagantly happy! She hadn't been able to eat or sleep. She had walked around in a trance.

Yet that wedding had made a great many people unhappy. The

boyfriend whom she'd jilted, needless to say; but also her mother and Ida, who had never so much as heard Joe's name before she stunned them with her news on an unannounced trip home. "Wait: I thought you were marrying Will," her mother had said. And, "You've known this person *how* long? He makes his living doing *what?*" And finally, "I just have to point out, Rebecca, that this is mighty convenient for him. A case where a man is so needful, where a wife would be so useful. Three little girls to take care of! And their mother nowhere in sight! I guess he *would* want to marry!"

Rebecca had accused her mother of doubting that anyone could love her. She had left the house in tears, slamming the door behind her, vowing not to return. " I never said... !" her mother called, trailing her down the driveway. "I only meant... Couldn't you first have a long engagement? What's your hurry?"

A question asked as well by people at Macadam—her faculty advisor and her history professor. Why sacrifice a college degree, they said, to marry a near-stranger thirteen years her senior? Why not wait till she graduated?

And on Joe's side, there were his daughters. Oh, his mother was ecstatic; you'd think the whole romance was her idea. And the other adults seemed delighted. But his daughters were stony-faced and resistant. They left Rebecca's chirpy remarks hanging foolishly in midair, and they found a million reasons to mention "our mama" in her presence. More than once, in those two weeks before the wedding, they had made Rebecca cry.

So many tears, now that she looked back! It hadn't been pure happiness after all. Part of that time, she'd been miserable.

But always there was Joe.

He drew her close and she pressed her face against his ropy brown throat. He called her his corn-fed girl, his creamy one, his beautiful blond milkmaid. (All those dairy-type references.) He wiped her eyes with his handkerchief that carried his smell of warm toast.

So was it the happiness or the misery that had made her lose those eight pounds?

Which, anyway, she had regained soon enough after the wedding.

Her mother and Aunt Ida were on the next subject by now—or the next two subjects. Her mother was saying that lately it seemed any chair she sat in was a struggle to get out of, and Ida was saying simultaneously that it wasn't only her vet who had retired but her doctor as well, and also her podiatrist, both of them replaced by mere whippersnapper youngsters. There was a pause, and then Ida said, "Old again"—announcing yet another convergence of topics. And they sighed and started off their next two conversational paths.

◎ *Anne Tyler's favorite book as a young girl was the children's classic,* The Little House, *by Virginia Lee Burton. She believes that it showed her "how the world worked, how the years flowed by and people altered and nothing could ever stay the same."*

That awareness of mutability in character, linked to an almost nostalgic longing for permanence, runs through the many wonderful worlds Tyler has created with her novels and short stories. Critics have praised her insightful portraits of middle-class lives, her vivid dialogue, and her well-wrought tales that invariably leave readers feeling satisfied that they have come to know her characters as intimately as it's possible to know anyone.

Tyler likes to keep her own personal details closer to the vest. She was born in Minneapolis in 1941 but moved with her family to North Carolina when she was six. Her parents were eager to raise their children in a community that lived according to ideal principles, and they found such a place among Quaker families in the North Carolina hills. They farmed together, shared community tasks, and taught the children communally. Tyler also attended a small public school nearby, where at the age of seven she wrote her first short stories—mostly about "lucky, lucky girls who got to go West in covered wagons."

Tyler graduated from Duke University at 19, benefiting from the guiding hand of writer Reynolds Price, who introduced her to his literary agent. Her first novel, If Morning Ever Comes, *was published when she was 23. Tyler had recently gotten married, to an Iranian psychiatrist named Taghi Modarressi, with whom she had two daughters. (Modarressi died in 1997.) The couple eventually settled in Baltimore, the backdrop for many of her novels, including* The Accidental Tourist, *which won the National Book Critics Circle Award in 1986 and was later made into a feature film. Her* Breathing Lessons *won the Pulitzer Prize in 1988.*

Tyler never goes on book tours. She grants only the rare e-mail interview. Instead, she prefers to let her writing, and her characters, speak for her. "What I hope for from a book— either one that I write or one that I read—is transparency," she has commented. "I want the story to shine through. I don't want to think of the writer."

Alice Hoffman

The Probable Future

What was a rose but the living proof of desire, the single best evidence of human longing and earthly devotion. But desire could be twisted, after all, and Jealousy was the name of a rose that did well in arid soils. Red Devil flourished where no other rose grew, at the edge of the garden, in shadows. In many ways, a rose resembled the human heart; some were wild, others were in need of constant care. Although many varieties had been transformed and tamed, no two were exactly alike. There were those that tasted like cherries and those that smelled like lemons. Some were vigorous, while others faded in a single day. Some grew in swamps, some needed bushels of fertilizer. Rose fossils dating back three and a half billion years had been found, but in all this time there had never been a blue rose, for the rose family did not possess that pigment. Gardeners have had to be satisfied with counterfeits: Blue Moon, with its mauve buds, or Blue Magenta, a wicked rambler that was actually violet and had to be cut back brutally to stop it from spreading where it wasn't wanted.

None of these false varieties grew in Elinor Sparrow's garden. She wanted a blue that was true, robin's-egg blue, delphinium blue, blue as the reaches of heaven. Clearly, she was a woman who didn't mind taking on an unattainable task. Other gardeners might have backed down from the rules of genetics, but not Elinor. She wasn't scared off by what others proclaimed impossible any more than she was bothered by the clouds of mosquitoes that rose at dusk at this time of year, as soon as the earth began to warm and the last of the snow had melted.

Elinor Sparrow hadn't cared about gardening until her husband's accident. The garden at Cake house, established hundreds of years earlier, had been neglected for decades. A few of the old roses Rebecca Sparrow had planted still managed to bloom among the milkweed and spiny nettles. The stone walls, carefully chinked by Sarah Sparrow, Rebecca's daughter, were still standing, and the wrought-iron gate put up by Elinor's own great-grandmother, Coral, had not rusted completely and was easily cleaned with boric acid and lye.

Elinor should have built her world around Jenny when Saul died in that accident on a road outside Boston, but instead she walked into the garden and she had never come out again. Oh, she'd gone grocery shopping, she'd passed her neighbors on Main Street on her way to the pharmacy, but all she truly wanted was to be alone. All she could bear was the comfort of earth between her fingers, the repetition of the tasks at hand. Here, at least, she could make something grow. Here what you buried arose once more, given the correct amounts of sunlight and fertilizer and rain.

Elinor Sparrow had brought forth record-breaking blooms in past growing seasons: scented damasks as big as a horse's hoof, rosa rugosas that would flower until January, Peace roses so glorious that upon several occasions thieves had tried to steal cuttings, until the wolfhound, Argus, whose canines were worn down to nubs, managed to scare the intruders away with a few deep woofs. Seeing all the greenery behind the stone walls, even in the month of March, when the buds were only beginning to form, no one would ever imagine how difficult it had been for Elinor to garden in this place. For two years after Saul died, nothing would grow, despite Elinor's best efforts. It may have been the salt on her skin, the bitterness in her heart. Whatever the reason, everything withered, even the roses that Rebecca Sparrow had planted. Elinor hired landscapers, but they failed to enlighten her and merely suggested that she use DDT and sulfur. She sent soil samples to the lab at MIT and was told there was nothing amiss that a little bonemeal and tender care couldn't correct.

One day, when Elinor was working in the garden, nearly defeated, thinking it might not be possible for her to go on, Brock Stewart, the town doctor, stopped by. Dr. Stewart still made house calls back then; the reason he was at Cake House was because Jenny, only twelve at the time, had called and asked that he come. Jenny had a long-drawn-out bout with the flu, accompanied by a hacking cough that wouldn't go away and headaches that were so bad she kept the room dark. She was only in sixth grade, but she had already learned to take care of herself.

"Where's your mother?" Dr. Stewart had asked after he'd examined Jenny. Why, the girl was quite feverish, and she didn't have a glass of water on her night table or a cold cloth for her forehead.

"My mother is in the garden." Jenny was a serious individual, even then. "It's the only thing she cares about, so I put a curse on it."

"Did you?" Dr. Stewart was a fine physician and he never overlooked a child's opinion. "What sort of curse?"

Jenny sat up in bed. She had meant to keep the curse secret, but she was so flattered by Dr. Brock's interest that she let him in on the intricacies of the hex.

Come here no more, not in day, not in evening, not in rain, not in sunshine.

Jenny smiled at the doctor, pleased by how solemnly he considered the enchantment. "I looked it up in a book in the library corner in our parlor. It's a verse that keeps the bees away. No garden can grow without them."

"I didn't know that."

As the town's only doctor, Brock Stewart was always amazed by the various ways people found to hurt each other, without even trying, it seemed. He was continually astounded by how fragile a human being was, yet how miraculously resilient; how it was possible to carry on through illness and hardship in the most unexpected ways.

"My father was the one who told me that bees dislike bad language," Jenny went on, her tongue loosened. "What they hate most of all is when somebody in a household dies. They often take off when that happens." Jenny's knotted hair looked perfectly black against her overheated skin. She was a very precise girl who hated flowers, dirt, earthworms, and disorder. She had Scotch-taped a row of her tiny paintings to the walls, intricate monkey-puzzle watercolors in which things fit together perfectly: rug and table, house and sky, mother and daughter.

"I see." Dr. Stewart wrote it all down. Children seemed to like when he did that, even the older ones; they could tell he was paying attention when he committed their comments to paper. "And is there a cure for this curse?"

"If someone dies or if the go-away verse is spoken aloud, the bees won't come back until you offer them cake. Anything sweet will do. And you have to invite them to come back. Politely. Like you mean it. Like you care."

Dr. Stewart phoned the pharmacy and asked them to deliver some antibiotics, then he patted Jenny's feverish head and went out to the garden. Elinor Sparrow was on her hands and knees, weeding a bed in which every shrub had turned mottled and leafless. She barely took notice of people anymore. She was too twisted up by her own terrible fate, far too wounded to pay attention to much of anything other than her empty garden.

"I see nothing's growing," Brock Stewart called out.

"Congratulations on stating the obvious." Elinor didn't like most people, but at least she respected Brock, so she didn't chase him off. Not right away. She had never once caught him in a lie, and that couldn't be said for many folks in town. "Do I get a bill for that opinion or is it free?"

"You've been cursed," Dr. Stewart informed his neighbor. "And you probably deserve it."

Every time the doctor saw Elinor he was reminded of the way she had looked at him on that icy evening when he had to tell her about Saul's accident. She had looked inside him then, as though searching for the truth. She was looking inside him now. Dr. Stewart was a tall man, and there were some children in town who were afraid of his height and his stern manner. But the ones who knew him well didn't fear him at all. They asked him for lollipops; they told him about what mattered most to them, curses and bees and forgiveness.

"You're overlooking all the important things, Elly. Just listen."

They stared at each other over the garden gate. Elinor Sparrow could not believe this man had the nerve to call her Elly, but she let that pass. She listened carefully. White clouds moved across the sky and the light was especially clear, with the luminous, milky quality out-of-town visitors always noticed.

"I don't hear anything." Elinor brushed the dirt from her hands and knees, annoyed.

"Precisely. No bees."

"No bees." Elinor felt like an idiot. Why hadn't she noticed before?

The silence was so obvious, the problem so apparent. "Who would have put a curse like that on me?"

Dr. Stewart shrugged. After all these years of being the only doctor in a small town, he knew enough not to place blame, especially when it resided so close by.

"Now that you know what's wrong, you can fix it. Here's how: Feed 'em cake." Dr. Stewart made this suggestion matter-of-factly, much as he would recommend aspirin for headaches or ginger ale and licorice syrup for stomachaches. "Then ask them to come back. And be polite when you do it. Their feelings have been hurt. And they're not the only ones, if you really want to know."

Elinor had gone directly to the kitchen once the doctor left. She searched the pantry until she found a week-old sponge cake, which she doused with brandy and cream. But before she could carry the platter outside, the doorbell rang. It was the delivery boy from the pharmacy, who dropped off Jenny's antibiotics, then rushed back to his car, making a hasty U-turn before Elinor could approach and accuse him of trespassing.

As Elinor Sparrow examined the vial of chalky penicillin, she realized something about her house. Cake House was even more silent than the garden was without bees. She had hurt their feelings, and she hadn't even known it. She had been caught in some sort of web that spun days into months, months into years. She understood exactly where the curse had begun. It was the damage she'd done, it was the way she'd turned away, it was the child left to fend for herself.

Jenny was half-asleep when Elinor came upstairs with her medicine.

"Take this and hurry up," Elinor said.

Jenny was so surprised to have her mother ministering to her that she quickly did as she was told.

"Now get out of bed and come with me."

Jenny threw on her bathrobe and followed, barefoot and confused. She thought of a dozen possibilities for her mother's sudden interest: the lake had overflowed, the pipes in the house had burst, the wasps in the attic had broken through the plasterboard. Surely, it must be a true emergency for her mother to think of her.

"I haven't been paying attention to things." They had stopped in the pantry, so that Elinor could fetch the sticky cake. Ants had crawled onto the plate, and the smell of the brandy was overwhelming. "Now I have to give this to the bees. I have to ask for their forgiveness and invite them to come back." She looked right at Jenny, her tangled hair, her wary expression. "I hope it's not too late."

Elinor took the cake outside. Before she had taken two steps, a bee had appeared to hover above her in the air.

"Was Dr. Stewart the one who told you about the bees?" Jenny was feverish, and being on her feet made her dizzy. She stayed on the porch and leaned against the railing. "I told him a secret, and he went and told you."

"Of course he did. Now let's hope it works."

As for Elinor, she felt light-headed as well. Like a fool, she had thrown something away, and now she was trying her best to get it back. The cake she was holding smelled like spring, a heady mix of pollen and honey, lilacs and brandy. Dozens of bees had begun to follow Elinor across the lawn. Perhaps there was a cure for some things: what was ruined, what was lost, what was all but thrown away.

"Please come into my garden."

Elinor pushed open the gate and the bees followed her inside, but Jenny stood where she was, stubborn, unforgiving.

"Come with me," Elinor said to her daughter.

By then, hundreds of bees were flying over Lockhart Avenue, skimming over the thorn bushes on Dead Horse Lane, buzzing through the forsythia and the laurel.

Jenny was hot from her fever and cold from the chill of the day. She realized that her mother hadn't thought to recommend that she put on shoes; Elinor wasn't that sort of mother, no matter what she might pretend. Jenny's toes had a tingling feeling, the sign of sure disaster. But which way was adversity? She could walk forward or could take a step back, or she could stay exactly where she was, unmoving, which is what she did on that day of a hundred bees. She did not make a move.

Nature—and roses in particular—looms large in Alice Hoffman's distinctive brand of magical realism. In The Probable Future—her 16th novel, sampled here—Hoffman likens the rose to the human heart, noting that "some were wild, others were in need of constant care." And like the human heart, some roses are hard to control: Elinor Sparrow, one of the protagonists of The Probable Future, strives to tame nature in the last years of her life through attempts, ultimately unsuccessful, to cultivate a blue rose.

The Probable Future tells the story of 13 generations of Sparrow daughters living in the small town of Unity, Massachusetts. Each daughter is endowed with a magical gift that is revealed to her only on her 13th birthday. The story centers on three generations of the family. Elinor Sparrow can literally smell a lie; her daughter, Jenny, can see people's dreams. Jenny's frustration with Elinor's indifference to her is a central theme of the book. It remains unresolved until circumstances with Jenny's own daughter, Stella (who can foretell how people will die), conspire to reunite mother, daughter, and granddaughter in the house where Jenny was raised.

Born in New York in 1952, Hoffman published her first novel, Property Of, at age 25. Since then she has made a career of writing modern-day parables, infused with her trademark brand of magic and potential.

"I always felt and still feel that fairy tales have an emotional truth that is so deep that there are few things that really rival [them]," she says. "I also like the whole idea of fairy tales and folk tales being a woman's domain, considered a lesser domain at the time they were told."

Billy Collins

Rooms

After three days of steady, inconsolable rain,
I walk through the rooms of the house
wondering which would be best to die in.

The study is an obvious choice
with its thick carpet and soothing paint,
its overstuffed chair preferable
to a doll-like tumble down the basement stairs.

And the kitchen has a certain appeal—
it seems he was boiling water for tea,
the inspector will offer, holding up the melted kettle.

Then there is the dining room,
just the place to end up facedown
at one end of its long table in a half-written letter

or the bedroom with its mix of sex and sleep,
upright against the headboard,
a book having slipped to the floor—
make it *Mrs. Dalloway,* which I have yet to read.
Dead on the carpet, dead on the tiles,
dead on the stone cold floor—

it's starting to sound like a ballad
sung in a pub by a man with a coal red face.

It's all the fault of the freezing rain
which is flicking against the windows,
but when it finally lets up
and gives way to broken clouds and a warm breeze,
when the trees stand dripping in the light,

I will quit these dark, angular rooms
and drive along a country road
into the larger rooms of the world,
so vast and speckled, so full of ink and sorrow—

a road that cuts through bare woods
and tangles of red and yellow bittersweet
these late November days.

And maybe under the fallen wayside leaves
there is a hidden nest of mice,
each one no bigger than a thumb,
a thumb with closed eyes,
a thumb with whiskers and a tail,
each one contemplating the sweetness of grass
and the startling brevity of life.

Born in New York City in 1941, Billy Collins may well be America's most popular living poet. His last three collections of poems broke sales records for poetry, and he appears regularly on National Public Radio. His work has been featured in the Pushcart Prize anthology and has been chosen several times for the annual "Best American Poetry" series. In 2001 Collins was named the 44th Poet Laureate of the United States, serving two terms. As Poet Laureate, he read his poem "The Names" at a special joint session of the United States Congress on September 6, 2002, held to remember the victims of the 9/11 attacks.

"Limpid, gently and consistently startling, more serious than they seem," John Updike wrote, Collins's poems "describe all the worlds that are and were and some others besides." The poems are remarkable for their deceptive simplicity and sly humor, yet—like "Rooms" from Nine Horses—they often deal with death. As Collins has put it, "There's one subject in lyric poetry—and that is that you have this existence and at the end of it you're going to experience non-existence."

Compare the two, he adds, and "you're struck with the fact that existence is full of particulars like a breadbox or a girl's ponytail or a cup of soup, whereas non-existence would seem to lack these particulars. So that the poems are kind of urgent recognitions or celebrations of the particular world around us that we are leaving as we speak."

TELL THE WORLD THIS BOOK WAS		
GOOD	BAD	SO-SO

Acknowledgments

Our heartfelt thanks go to Jeremy Janes, who conceived, edited, and championed this volume. Sincere appreciation, too, to Helena Janes and Luke Janes for their generous editorial assistance, which included furnishing their insights into Jeremy's life and character.

Bill Novelli and Cathy Ventura-Merkel were instrumental in steering the project to AARP Books. At Sterling Publishing, Inc., Charlie Nurnberg and Steve Magnuson gave the book their unstinting support throughout.

We are also indebted to Gail Sheehy for her meditation on the value of a life fully lived, to book designer Lynn Phelps for gracefully framing the subject, and to Carl Lehmann-Haupt for his creative guidance. Roberta Conlan lent her poetic touch to many of the author profiles, which were researched and written by Jessica Allen, Ed Dwyer, Antony Shugaar, Bob Somerville, and Jane Sunderland. Kevin Craig contributed his typographical perspicacity.

We owe an especially large debt of gratitude to the level-headed Lisa Thomas, whose resourcefulness, tenacity, and intelligence were pivotal on the permissions and editorial fronts. Theresa Rademacher provided crucial support throughout the life of the project as well.

We tender our sincere thanks to every member of this talented team.

—*Hugh Delehanty, Editor-in-Chief, AARP Publications*
Allan Fallow, Managing Editor, AARP Books

About Gail Sheehy

Cultural observer Gail Sheehy has applied the power of experience to build a rich and varied career. Her book *Passages,* named one of the 10 most influential books of our time in a Library of Congress survey, revolutionized the way millions of people approach their lives. It was a *New York Times* bestseller for more than three years and has been reprinted in 28 languages.

Her latest work, *Sex and the Seasoned Woman: Pursuing the Passionate Life,* chronicles boomer outlooks on sex, dating, new dreams, divorce, remarriage, spiritual growth, and the prospect of living more passionately in the second half of our lives. Her previous books include *The Silent Passage, Hillary's Choice,* and *Middletown, America.*

As a literary journalist, Sheehy was one of the original contributors to *New York* magazine. A contributing editor to *Vanity Fair* since 1984, she won the Washington Journalism Review Award for Best Magazine Writer in America for her in-depth character portraits of national and world leaders, including Bill and Hillary Clinton, Newt Gingrich, Mikhail Gorbachev, Saddam Hussein, Margaret Thatcher, and both Bush presidents.

Sheehy is a seven-time recipient of the New York Newswomen's Club Front Page Award for distinguished journalism—most recently for her *Vanity Fair* article, "September Widows." She has also won a National Magazine Award, as well as the Anisfield-Wolf Book Award in Race Relations for *Spirit of Survival.*

About Jeremy Janes

Trained in literary appreciation at Oxford University, England, where he read Modern Languages, Jeremy Francis Ralph Janes emigrated from England to California in 1965 and earned a master's degree in comparative literature from the University of California at Davis in 1968. After working as a teacher and a community-outreach specialist in California, Janes became the communications director for AARP Wisconsin and served in that capacity from 2000 until 2006. He also wrote numerous articles about film, literature, and politics for various magazines and newspapers, among them *The Los Angeles Times, Mother Jones,* and the *Santa Barbara Independent.*

Though Jeremy Janes did not see this anthology come to fruition—he died in 2006—his delight in the written word lives on in his selection of these works. He designed the book to be a grateful celebration of the joys as well as the realities of life in later years—and a call to live life to its fullest at every stage.

Credits